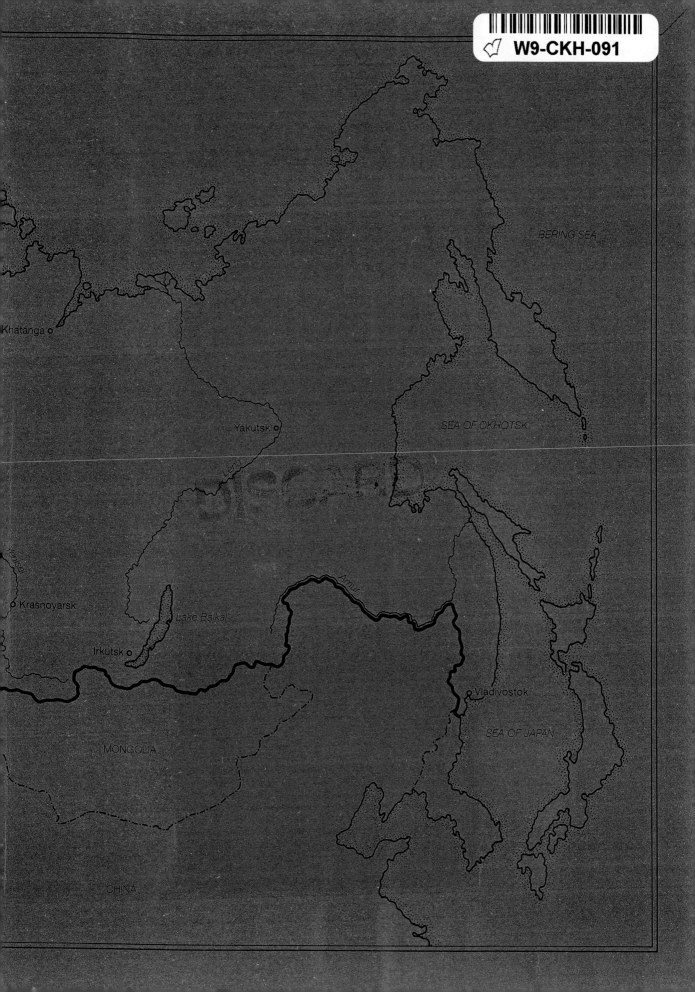

BERING SEA

Khatanga o

Yakutsk o

Lena

SEA OF OKHOTSK

Yenisei

o Krasnoyarsk

Lake Baikal

Amur

Irkutsk o

Vladivostok

MONGOLIA

SEA OF JAPAN

CHINA

RED EMPIRE

RED EMPIRE

The Forbidden History of the USSR

*Gwyneth Hughes and
Simon Welfare*

With an Introduction by
Robert Conquest

ST. MARTIN'S PRESS
New York

004431

Text and captions © Gwyneth Hughes and Simon Welfare 1990
Introduction © Robert Conquest 1990

All rights reserved. For information, write:
Scholarly and Reference Division,
St. Martin's Press, Inc., 175 Fifth Avenue,
New York, N.Y. 10010

First published in the United States of America in 1990

Printed in Great Britain

ISBN 0–312–05295–2

Library of Congress Cataloging-in-Publication Data applied for.

Contents

Acknowledgements

This book is dedicated to the production team of the *Red Empire* television series, both East and West

Picture Credits: *David King Collection* half title, 12 (all), 13 (all), 16, 17, 18 (all), 35, 36 (all), 38 top, 39 (all), 40 (all), 41, 42, 43, 44, 45 bot., 47 (all), 48 (all), 49, 51, 52 mid. and bot., 56 top, 57 (all), 58, 59, 60 (all), 61 (all), 63, 65 (all), 66, 67 bot. l. and r., 68, 69 top, 70 bot., 71 (all), 72, 73, 75, 76, 77, 78 (all), 80 (all), 81 bot., 85, 87 top, 88, 89, 90, 91, 92, 93, 94 top, 95 (all), 97 (all), 99 (all), 100, 101, 102, 103 mid. and bot., 108 (all), 110, 111 r., 113 top, 116 (all), 117 (all), 119 top, 121, 122 (all), 123, 124 (all), 125 (all), 126 top, 127 bot., 144, 145 (all), 146, 147 (all), 148, 150 top l. and bot., 152 (all), 153 (all), 154 top, 155 bot., 157, 158, 160 l., 162 top, 166, 167 (all), 168, 178; *Robert Conquest* 7; *Robert Hunt Library* 33 top; *Topham* frontispiece, 33 bot., 52 top, 54 bot., 55, 56 bot., 127 top, 131 bot. r., 134 bot., 173, 176 top, 182, 182 top, 184, 185, 186 top l., 195 (all), 200; *Tass* 67 top, 69 bot., 81 top, 82, 94 bot., 105 (all), 111 l., 130, 156, 160 r., 161, 162 bot., 163, 174, 190 top, 194 top, 196 (all), 197 r., 199; *Roger Viollet* 70 top, 83 (all), 84 (all), 87 bot., 103 top, 131 bot. l., 135 (all), 154 bot., 164, 176 bot., 197 i.; *Arkady Vaksberg* 79; *Bridgeman Art Library* 113 bot., 114; *Frank Spooner/GAMMA* 118; *Rex Features/SIPA* 119 bot., 150 top r., 155 top, 172, 181, 183 bot., 186 top r. and bot., 187, 191 bot., 193, 194 bot.; *Associated Press* 120, 180 bot. r.; *Network* 126 bot.; *Ullstein* 131 top, 149; *Popperfoto* 132, 165 (all), 169, 180 top and bot. l., 189 top, 198 (all); *Novosti* 141 top; *Keston College* 188 (all); *Mirror Group Newspapers* 189 bot.; *Weidenfeld & Nicolson Archives* 8, 21, 24, 29, 38 bot., 45 top, 54 top, 115 (all), 138 bot., 142, 170 (all), 171

Maps drawn by Richard Natkiel Associates, based on maps in *Atlas of Soviet History* by Martin Gilbert

Introduction
by Robert Conquest

The authors of this book have asked me to make this introduction as personal as possible – doubtless as an illustration of how a historian seeking the facts copes with a system intent on concealing them.

I was born just after the July Days, which saw the Bolsheviks' first fumbling attempt to take power. Thus I and my generation both preceded and outlasted traditional Sovietism. As I write, survivors even include Lazar Kaganovich, Stalin's chief henchman, who joined the Party in 1911, and became a member of the Central Committee in 1922.

I first visited the Soviet Union in 1937. The realities of Stalin's rule, including many registered in this book, were largely secret: for most of us it was socialist, anti-fascist, therefore good. I had also read the Russian classics – especially Pushkin, Dostoievsky, Chekhov. A remarkable and richly talented culture was shown, and remained strongly in my consciousness though in a sense this gave a different image, a different message, from that of the Communists.

Anyway, when I got off the train in Leningrad, I did not expect the Soviet Union to be an advanced country. Russia had, so we

Robert Conquest in Moscow in 1989.

7

felt, been so backward that even the transition to socialism could hardly be expected to have produced much effect yet.

I missed what was hidden, I saw what was shown, but I did not actually hallucinate like the Sovietophiles aptly characterized by Malcolm Muggeridge: Quakers applauding tank parades, feminists ecstatic about women bowed down under a hundredweight of coal, architects gazing in awe at gimcrack buildings, just erected and already crumbling away. I was a little surprised, on first leaving my hotel, to be at once approached by a spiv wanting to buy my watch and my shirt – a tattered affair in which I had been tramping for weeks. I am even more surprised thinking about it now, for, as I learned later, in 1937 any contact with foreigners was automatic grounds for arrest on an espionage charge. In fact, I had arrived during the very worst period of the Terror. As Nadezhda Mandelstam, widow of the purged poet, wrote, when the killings became secret, they became worse.

That summer of 1937 was also the time of a very large tourist influx into the Soviet Union. Opting for one trip in Leningrad, it was odd to find myself driving over to the Peter Paul fortress with two Germans – members of the Hitler Youth. I went on to Moscow, where I was approached by a student sour about the regime. I was not a good enough Marxist for the thought of denouncing him even to cross my mind: perhaps he was a provocateur anyway, but perhaps he was risking his life. In the

4 July 1917. Demonstrators on the Nevsky Prospect in Petrograd scatter in confusion after being fired upon. The July Days 'saw the Bolsheviks' first fumbling attempt to take power'.

Ukraine I was taken to a collective farm, doubtless the Potemkin kolkhoz 'October Revolution' then usually shown to foreign visitors. It was not very impressive even so, unlike the finest kolkhoz ever seen, in Lillian Hellman's Hollywood film *North Star*, made during a period of American–Soviet friendship. I swam in the Black Sea at Odessa among a crowd of locals dressed in squalid underwear. Then, even odder to think of now, I went all alone by train from Odessa to what at that time was the Soviet–Romanian border at Tiraspol, changing halfway to a slow local. It was crammed with peasants, but I had got on to the luggage rack and made myself comfortable. After a time the conductor asked me to get down. In German, via a Yiddish-speaking passenger, I resisted, until it turned out he was offering me a seat in the guard's van. I recount all this partly in a nostalgic vein, but also to recall how unrigorous control over visitors was then, especially as compared with late Stalinism, or even with the 1970s.

The creature comforts, for the visitor, did not strike me as at all bad at a plain level: but that fortnight in the Soviet Union was part of a two-month bummel round Europe with my friend John Blakeway (left in Finland, met again in Romania). In fact the Soviet stretch was the most expensive, a pound a day. Elsewhere it was Lappish huts, a portside khan in the slums of Galata, a cheap brothel in Bucharest, the hard deck of an Italian tramp steamer. On arrival in Paris, we were welcomed by my then girlfriend, a fellow undergraduate of, as I recall, enchanting beauty. John, left on his own, wandered the streets. In the Rue de la Sorbonne he passed a couple of students sitting in the gutter, ostentatiously begging from passers-by. Short of money himself, he sat down and joined them. They turned out to be Bulgarians, and when we all got together I became friendly with one of them – Ivan Ranchev – and at the same time very interested in Bulgaria and things Bulgarian, though at this time, and for several more years, I had not even a rudimentary knowledge of any Slav language.

In 1938 I lost much of my interest in politics, in part because of girl trouble (the same girl). But I still nourished some delusions about the Soviet Union and its socialism. This was due mainly to the failure of many of those whose duty it was to discover and transmit the truth. Soviet official statistics were accepted; Soviet official denials were accepted too. The few truth-tellers, like Muggeridge, appeared to be cranks compared with the phalanx of imposing establishment authorities like the deans of Western sociology, Sydney and Beatrice Webb, or the grand old man of British Russianists, Sir Bernard Pares, backed up by venal journalists like Walter Duranty, and duped ambassadors like Joseph Davies. No doubt I and others should have been more sceptical. But the pro-Soviet falsification had sunk in deep. As Arthur Koestler writes, London swarmed with 'thousands of painters and writers and doctors and lawyers and debutantes chanting a diluted version of the Stalinist line'. When Hitler invaded Russia, this mood revived.

During the war, I chanced briefly to be acting adjutant at my regiment's Infantry Training Centre. A War Office circular arrived, asking for officers for crash courses in the Eastern European languages. I put in for Bulgarian and, as few opted for it, was accepted.

'What's all this about your going on a four-month course,' howled the Colonel.

'You remember, Sir, you signed it ...'

Eventually, in the late summer of 1944, another survivor of the course and I were flown in to Bulgaria. This was, of course, for liaison with the Bulgarians, now fighting the Germans in Macedonia; but their armies were soon part of the Soviet Third Ukrainian Front, so I was technically under Russian command. There was much unofficial contact, with groups of Red Army men met by choice in krutchmas, on the road, in Sofia – often ending in devastating booze-ups. Official contact too: I remember going with an RAF Group Captain to the funeral of a Soviet general who had been killed when RAF fighters had shot up his column owing to a map-reading error. My colleague offered apologies, and showed on a map how the layout of bridges, roads and rivers of the area attacked resembled that of the true target. The Soviet commander waved the map aside and told us not to feel too bad about it, as such things happened all the time. This was so very contrary to the usual Soviet habit of extracting the maximum guilt from Allied representatives even for far lesser, or quite imaginary offences, that I saw it at once as the natural Russian generosity, otherwise masked or distorted by the Party. In general, I was much taken with the reckless, devil-may-care attitude of all ranks, and their rough attitude to stuffy political officers and secret policemen, at least in the front areas, though this petered out as the fighting receded into Serbia.

Ivan Ranchev had been among the first people I came across in Sofia, and he was astonished that I now spoke excellent Bulgarian. Though highly non-political, he was optimistic about the new Communist-supported coalition government. But it soon became obvious that the Communist-controlled police ministry. was behaving atrociously, under direct Soviet instructions, and I date my final revulsion from the Stalinist system to early 1945.

As the war ended, there was a brief period of comparative political liberty. Ivan, who was now a journalist, one day came to me with a long factual analysis of the Bulgarian press. I gave it to our political mission. They then asked the military to transfer me to them as press attaché. When I was demobilized in 1946 I was offered the job as a civilian, so I went back to Sofia, managing to get John Blakeway, just demobilized from the Indian Army, as my assistant. I left in 1948, smuggling Ivan out, in circumstances I will one day recount. I thus saw the whole dreadful process of the Stalinization of a country. Back in London, in the Foreign Office, they allotted me to the newly formed Information Research Department, established by Ernest Bevin to provide factual briefing in the new struggle against the world-wide Stalinist political and propaganda offensive, and thus I became involved in Soviet studies proper.

It will be seen that it was through a concatenation of accidents that I eventually found myself in the Soviet field. Perhaps this gave me an especially sharp insight into the role of accident in history, as against theory-predicted causality. Indeed, I suppose I might maintain that the above set of events affected history itself. For example, it was my book *The Great Terror* which, as he said in a Senate speech and elsewhere, first roused Senator Henry 'Scoop' Jackson's deep interest in Soviet matters. Jackson was, more than anyone else, the force which held the Democrats (or enough of them) together in implanting a firm American attitude in the so-called Cold War. Thus, John Blakeway chancing to run across Ivan Ranchev in a Latin Quarter gutter in 1937 may have saved the West – and even saved the world from nuclear war! But I fear there is no way of testing this hypothesis.

Over the years from 1948 to 1956, I learned a great deal. I did not at this stage speak Russian (I still speak it poorly), but I could read it reasonably well. I was attached for a time to the UK Delegation to the United Nations in New York, attending the minuscule meetings of the Security Council, and the vast swarm of the General Assembly (where I once sat next to Vyshinsky), drafting some of Barbara Castle's devastating replies to Soviet attacks in the Social and Economic Committee, and so on.

I was even published in *Pravda* . . . well, in 1951 Herbert Morrison, the then Foreign Secretary, said to Stalin that speeches and articles of Soviet leaders were printed in the British press, and that the opposite should also be true but wasn't. Stalin said *Pravda* would publish, without cuts, whatever Morrison cared to send in. I helped draft the article, not extreme but full of good stuff about freedom of speech, and containing such remarks as 'If you hear someone at your door at 4 am in England, it's the milkman.' It was indeed published uncut, an event unique in Soviet life for the next thirty-five years. It caused a sensation in Moscow, but was answered next day: Morrison (*Pravda* said) wanted freedom of speech in the USSR for 'those who had killed Kirov'. Well, actually, they were the only people who had it . . .

But in the main I became interested in the suppressed material, the recent history of the USSR. I felt increasing horror at what was going on, and what had been going on, there. And even greater horror at the success of the Stalinist campaign of falsification, not merely in the Soviet Union, but also in the West,

Retouching history. *From the first, Soviet propagandists demonstrated that, even if the camera never lies, photographs can.*

BELOW *Stalin is said to have ordered the removal of his rival Leon Trotsky from this famous picture of Lenin addressing troops about to depart for the Polish front in Sverdlov Square, Moscow, on 5 May 1920. In this version, only recently published in the Soviet Union, Trotsky and his brother-in-law Lev Kamenev are seen standing on the right of the podium.*

LEFT *After Stalin had disposed of them, Trotsky and Kamenev were painted out of the picture.*

RIGHT *The picture has been most often cropped like this by Soviet picture editors to show Lenin running the revolution single-handed.*

ABOVE LEFT AND RIGHT *This picture was taken in April 1925. It shows (left to right) Lashevich, Frunze, Smirnov, Rykov, Voroshilov, Stalin, Skrypnik, Bubnov and Ordzhonikidze. The same photograph, published twenty-four years later, has been retouched and re-arranged to suggest that the group included only four people: Frunze, Voroshilov, Stalin and Ordzhonikidze. The others have been airbrushed out of history.*

RIGHT ABOVE AND BELOW *Painting and cropping have both been used to alter this picture of a meeting of the Council of People's Commissars at the Kremlin in 1922. In the original, Kamenev and Rykov, who were both purged by Stalin, are standing behind Lenin. Trotsky is sitting at the table, fourth from right. In the doctored photograph, Kamenev and Rykov have been crudely replaced by a piece of curtain and a screen, while the right-hand side of the picture has been cropped to exclude Trotsky. The retoucher has also been at work on the left-hand side, although no one seems to have been deliberately erased.*

where the voices of truth were commonly ignored, or slandered. I found that I was assembling a great many suppressed facts, or making deductions in the absence of such facts, and in 1956 I resigned to take a fellowship at the London School of Economics and write my first books on the Soviet Union. I had already published two books – a collection of poems and a science fiction novel, so felt I was adequately equipped on the technical side.

These first books on Soviet subjects were *Power and Policy in the USSR*, on the hidden political struggle within the leadership; and *The Soviet Deportation of Nationalities* (later rewritten as *The Nation Killers*) on the Crimean Tatars and other peoples transported east en masse in the 1940s: each the first treatment of its theme.

Meanwhile, I had academic appointments, including a year as Lecturer in English and Visiting Poet at the University of Buffalo. And I produced other books including – at his request – a verse translation of Solzhenitsyn's *Prussian Nights*. The major 'blank spots' in Soviet history were, of course, the 'great terror' of 1936–38, and the terror against the peasantry in 1930–33. I covered these in *The Great Terror* and *The Harvest of Sorrow*.

In the Soviet Union my work was largely ignored, though I seldom met a Soviet official or scholar who had not read *The Great Terror* either in *samizdat* or in an émigré Russian edition published in Florence. Occasionally I was attacked in the Soviet press – as recently as 1985, I was unfavourably compared with Dr Goebbels.

The collapse of the traditional Soviet order included – in fact was to a large degree the result of – the collapse of the whole fabric of falsification. As this affected me personally (or is illustrated by that), it was a matter of the past two years. In 1988, favourable references to *The Great Terror* began to appear. Early in 1989, *Moscow News* printed a full-page interview with me, with praise for *The Great Terror* which 'had come by unofficial channels to the Soviet Union and was soon widely distributed in intellectual circles'.

In April the editor of *Neva*, People's Deputy Boris Nikolsky, announced that he would publish the whole book, in instalments, not only as 'by far the most serious work' on the period but also because it exemplified *Neva's* commitment to 'a legal state and the deepening of democratization'. It began to come out in September 1989, prefaced by an interview in which *Neva* wrote, 'Some of us read your book many years ago by night, at risk, as you understand. It struck us not only by its strength in exposure of truth, its multitude of facts, its penetration, but also by a sort of noble moral position, wisdom and compassionate decency.'

Novy Mir now published the long chapter from *The Harvest of Sorrow* on the famine. It commented:

We wish to emphasize a characteristic of his historical style not often found in the works of Western sovietologists. The analysis of facts produced by R. Conquest is exact and merciless; but his account is completely free of either positivist indifference or political malice. The enumeration of and confrontation with objective facts is kept clearly distinct from the author's own voice – full of sadness and sympathy for the great misfortunes of, one would have said, a people wholly foreign to him. We, the compatriots of the innocents who perished, must be grateful to the English historian.

Other excerpts appeared in *Rodina*, and are to do so elsewhere. *Rodina* commented, 'The author never departs from the documented base ... the reality itself which is reconstructed here works on the feelings more strongly than extreme fictional fantasy.'

Other Soviet periodicals interviewed me. The literary weekly *Knizhnoe Obozrenie* remarked, 'Conquest's book, whose theme is our cruel sufferings, does not kill the soul, but strengthens it, because it is written with love and hope.' Meanwhile there were odd comments in many other articles – in *Nedelya* praise for a more recent book of mine, *Stalin and the Kirov Murder*; in *Literaturnaya Gazeta*, a historian remarking, 'When you read Conquest, you feel him very close to us.'

Meanwhile, I visited the Soviet Union – for the first time since 1937 – and was warmly welcomed. I addressed the editorial boards of *Novy Mir*, *Neva*, *Voprosy Istorii*, *Druzhba Narodov*; I was asked to go on television, to speak at the Institute of History of the USSR, and so on ...

I record all this not, or not entirely, out of vanity, though public vindication on this scale is a rare event in intellectual history, and it would be absurd for me to deny a natural gratification. But, more generally, this is no more than one sign, if a very striking one, of the surrender of falsehood to truth, of the repudiation of the fearful interim of terror and lies.

What I now find in the Soviet Union, and not only in intellectual circles, is a profound hatred, long repressed, for a system which had forced people not only to accept, but to pretend enthusiasm for, this dull and miserable array of distortions and fantasies. One thing none of us could have been sure of was – had the long years of terror and indoctrination succeeded in destroying the people's spirit, in crippling it morally and intellectually? For such a series of numbing blows at the mind and the heart was totally without precedent, and we could not know the result.

But now it is clear that though the scars are still livid on the nation's flesh, the whole mad and murderous enterprise was, after all, a failure. The future of Russia, and of the other countries of the Soviet Union, cannot be predicted, and it may be that there are severe trials ahead. But, whatever happens, the human foundation remains sound. In this book, readers can see something of what the people had to endure.

1 Revolutionaries

The mines of Siberia are notorious to this day for their harsh climate and dangerous working conditions. One cold spring day in April 1912, a nineteen-year-old goldminer called Moisei Muravnik was among five thousand men, women and children who marched down the main street of their snowbound frontier settlement to protest. The miners had been on strike for a month at the pits run by the Lena Gold Mining Association, in protest at their atrocious standard of living. Their demonstration was orderly and good-humoured.

What happened next was described to the Imperial Parliament by the Minister of the Interior, Makarov. He said: 'The soldiers, only 110 men and without reserves, were alarmed and, fearful of an onrush, demanded orders to fire ...'

Two hundred people died, and many hundreds more were injured. Moisei Muravnik, now ninety-nine and living in a Moscow Home for Communist Party Veterans, remembers: 'We couldn't believe they would really fire. There was blood in the snow, women and children hurt. It was the first time I had ever seen a shooting.'

Factory owners in tsarist Russia, at fire extinguisher tests in St Petersburg. Men like these, soon to become bogeymen of the revolution, prospered on the eve of the First World War. After centuries of backwardness, industrialization was expanding rapidly. Russia was the fifth largest industrial power in the world – a major producer of steel, machinery and rubber goods, thanks to the almost insatiable demand for galoshes caused by the Russian winter.

A memorial to the 200 victims of the Lena goldfield massacre in Siberia. The goldfield was not alone in taking its name from the Lena River: so did Vladimir Ilyich Ulyanov, whose revolutionary name was – Lenin.

The horror of the Lena goldfield massacre transformed the young miner into a fervent revolutionary, and raised a hurricane of protest which tore across the empire, right into the capital city of St Petersburg. Hundreds of thousands of people went on sympathy strikes. Suddenly the mines of Siberia seemed not so far away from the splendid imperial court of Tsar Nicholas II, Emperor and Autocrat of all the Russias for the past twenty years.

The last emperor had come to the throne in 1896 at the age of twenty-six, tortured by self-doubt. 'I am not prepared to be a tsar. I never wanted to be one. I know nothing of the business of ruling,' he told his future brother-in-law Grand Duke Alexander. 'What is going to happen to me? To all of Russia?'

Half a million people had travelled to Moscow for his coronation, in the majestic Cathedral of the Assumption inside the walled citadel of the Kremlin. Poor, illiterate, devout, they had emerged from the forests and the steppes of Mother Russia, riding on the railway trains which were now opening up their vast empire. They congregated in the summer heat at Khodynka field in Moscow, hoping for a glass of beer and a glimpse of their 'little

ABOVE *Factory workers, like this group manning the barricades in St Petersburg, were at the forefront of a series of strikes and riots in 1905 which threatened the Tsar's authority. In January, troops fired on marchers petitioning the Tsar for improved wages and living conditions. Almost 200 were killed and many wounded on what became known as 'Bloody Sunday'.*

ABOVE *Women hauling barges on the Volga. In 1905, decades of resentment came to a head as the peasants set out to seize land they believed to be theirs by right.*

RIGHT *Almost half a century after the formal abolition of serfdom, most peasants were still in hock to the landowners. Primitive conditions and an unpredictable climate meant that many could not afford to feed themselves from one harvest to another: in 1891, hundreds of thousands had died in a famine.*

father'. When they heard that free coronation mugs were on offer there was a stampede. The official inquiry found that 1389 people died.

For his superstitious Russian subjects, there was another omen suggesting the last tsar's reign might be less than glorious. He married just a month after the death of his father, so his betrothed arrived in Moscow in the black of ceremonial mourning.

The bride was a German princess, Alexandra of Hesse-Darmstadt, one of Queen Victoria's forty grandchildren. Most of the crowned heads of Europe were related to each other. But they had yet to notice that their old imperial world was hurtling inexorably towards the flames of a pitiless war. Nicholas Romanov, the richest man in the world, had further to fall than any of them.

His cousin Kaiser Wilhelm of Germany did the matchmaking, introducing the shy young tsar to the austerely beautiful Princess Alix. It was a true love match. Nicholas was a devoted husband and loving father, especially when after four daughters Alexandra finally presented him with an heir to the throne. They christened the baby boy Alexei.

Clapped in irons. The activities of the Okhrana – the tsarist secret police – were one factor behind the 1905 protesters' demand for greater civil and political rights.

Tsar Nicholas II and his Empress Alexandra at the Kremlin, Moscow, in June 1913 for celebrations marking the 300th anniversary of the Romanov family's imperial rule. One eyewitness, who saw the eight-year-old Tsarevich being carried, wrote: 'As the procession paused ... I clearly heard exclamations of sorrow at the sight of this poor helpless child, the heir to the throne of the Romanovs.'

LEFT *The creation of the State Duma, or parliament, seen here during the religious service to mark its opening session in May 1906, was the Tsar's response to the 1905 troubles. Prime Minister Peter Stolypin began a programme of agricultural reforms designed to encourage enterprise and hard work among the more go-ahead peasants.*

But the child had inherited the crippling haemophilia which ran through the closely related families of European royalty. If he cut himself, he might bleed for weeks, and a knock could cause agonizingly painful bruises and swellings. Teams of doctors wrung their hands. Nothing could help the suffering child on whom the future of the Romanov dynasty depended. His mother was in despair.

So Alexandra barely noticed the humiliating war with Japan, or the consequent massive strikes and bloody riots of 1905, which swirled about the cities and the countryside outside the walls of the family's eight palaces. She was a mother, obsessed with the danger to her baby's life. As tsarism tottered on its foundations, as Nicholas was forced to give unthinkable concessions to the growing revolutionary movement, Alexandra sought help from a succession of folk healers and charlatans.

Among them was a wandering Siberian holy man called Rasputin. He had a greasy beard, staring eyes, and a reputation as a drinker and a womanizer. But the first time he laid hands on the tiny Tsarevich, he calmed the boy and the bleeding eased. Alexandra was overwhelmed with gratitude. For the next twelve years Grigory Rasputin was to be her chief source of spiritual succour and support.

As the Tsarevich grew, his illness was kept secret from a society which was being transformed. In those last years before the First World War, Russia was industrializing at a faster rate than any

ABOVE *Thanks to Azerbaijan's gushing wells, Russia's oil industry was second only to that of the United States in 1913. Overseas investors, like Nobel of Sweden, the owners of the rigs in this photograph, were important to the Russian economy and much missed after the revolution.*

LEFT *The Okhrana searching a train for illegal literature at the Finland Station in St Petersburg. One book not on the banned list was* Das Kapital *by Karl Marx. When it was published in Russia in 1872, it was deemed too academic to be subversive.*

A group of exiles in Siberia. Exile for political dissenters has a long tradition in Russia Lenin spent three years in Siberia from 1897; Stalin was also sent there.

other country in Europe. More and more, its people were drawn to the cities by the prospects of work in the huge new factories. They needed the money, but they did not like the long days, the dirt, the danger, the overcrowded and filthy hostels.

Added to the economic pressure was a political time bomb. The Russian Empire covered one sixth of the world's surface, reigning over scores of ethnic groups and a population of 130 million people. From Georgian princelings in the south to nomadic Muslims in the east, the peoples of the empire were beginning to sniff the heady air of nationalism.

The Romanov dynasty had ruled this vast land since 1613. The three-hundredth anniversary was celebrated in Moscow with spectacular pomp and pageantry, and immense crowds turned out to wave and shout their greetings. Among the sightseers was Nikolai Smernov, a working-class Muscovite schoolboy who climbed up into a tree near Pushkin Square to get a better view of the tossing plumes on the horses and the fine uniforms of the imperial guard. 'I remember thinking: the Tsar is so far above us, and we are here below,' he says. Within four years Nikolai was to become a revolutionary, building barricades in those same streets.

The year after the anniversary added a new and deadly ingredient to the cauldron of trade union grumblings and nationalist discontent simmering in the old empire.

In August 1914 the world went to war.

All over Europe a wave of patriotism swept millions into massive armies of helpless cannon fodder. There were small voices

*'The Russian Royal House':
a cartoonist's comment on
Rasputin's rumoured hold
over the Tsar and Tsarina.
The press had a field day with
lurid cartoons and gossip
about Alexandra and the
Siberian holy man.*

raised against the slaughter. Vladimir Lenin was among those
who sat in exile, at coffee tables in Geneva and Zurich, and
watched in despair as his cherished dream of international
proletarian solidarity drowned in the mire of the trenches.

At first Russia welcomed the war, and cheered the Tsar, and
marched off to the front with head held high. But the truth was
that the country was disastrously ill-prepared. By the end of the
first week of hostilities, the front line was running out of

ammunition. Few of the soldiers had decent boots or food, and a million of them had no rifles. Men waited for their comrades to fall and took their guns.

The shambles was inexcusable. The Russian high command had had ten years in which to prepare for war: ten years since they had been taught a humiliating and bitter lesson in the war with Japan. Those ten years had been wasted by a Tsar who was unhappy with the whole idea of modernization, by politicians who could not or would not persuade him, and by generals for whom life was cheap.

When the death toll reached four million, War Minister Polivanov told his alarmed colleagues: 'I place my trust in the impenetrable spaces, impassable mud and the mercy of Saint Nicholas Mirlikisky, Protector of Holy Russia.'

It was the summer of 1915, and the Tsar responded by doing a brave but foolhardy thing. He sacked his top general and appointed himself Commander-in-Chief of the Russian armed forces. All his advisers tried to dissuade him. They were afraid he would end up taking the personal blame for future military disasters, and they were proved right. But the Tsar was determined. He went off to the front to run the war.

At home, the war was increasingly unpopular. In the Azerbaijani capital of Baku, the British vice-consul Ranald MacDonnell saw women lying on the rails to stop the troop trains moving. In the faraway Central Asian province of Kazakhstan, a bloody revolt broke out against conscription.

St Petersburg had been patriotically renamed Petrograd to make it sound more Russian, but there was little to be proud of: wages were falling, queues growing, there was no firewood and

ABOVE *Russian prisoners of war after the Battle of Tannenberg. The first months of World War I were disastrous for the Russians. More than a quarter of their army had been killed, captured or wounded by the end of 1914.*

OPPOSITE PAGE *Soldiers of the 23rd Artillery Brigade from Gatchina pictured at a resting station on Lake Baikal on their way to the front, where the scene was usually less cheerful: ammunition, food and equipment were in short supply.*

ABOVE *Russian and German troops fraternizing in no-man's-land: a sign of the growing movement against the war.*

not much to eat. Endless Cabinet reshuffles meant that nobody seemed to be in control. In two years, there were four prime ministers, four ministers of war and six ministers of internal affairs.

In the Tsar's absence at the front, the Tsarina was in charge, and since Rasputin was as important to her as ever, they made a formidable pair of Aunt Sallies. In the eyes of the beleaguered capital, she was a German and he was a libertine. The streets were alive with rumours of treachery and sexual scandal. A young noblewoman, Zinaida Purishkevich, wrote:

'It was about this time that I first heard people speaking of the emperor and empress with open animosity and contempt. The word revolution was uttered more openly and more often; soon it could be heard everywhere ... Rasputin, Rasputin, Rasputin, it was like a refrain: his mistakes, his shocking personal conduct, his mysterious power ... This power was tremendous; it was like dusk enveloping all our world, eclipsing the sun.'

Zinaida's brother, Vladimir Purishkevich, was a right-wing extremist. On the night of 16 December 1916, Prince Yusupov and the Romanov Grand Duke Dmitri Pavlovich enticed Rasputin into a trap and killed him. Purishkevich helped the killers to throw him off the Petrovsky Bridge into the river Neva. The

corpse which floated up under the ice downstream had been shot, stabbed and poisoned: even so, some say the victim was still alive when he entered the water.

The poet Alexander Blok wrote: 'The bullet which killed him reached the very heart of the ruling dynasty.' The Romanov tsars had just ten weeks left.

The assassins were the toast of Petersburg. The Tsarina's own sister called down blessings on the pair for their patriotic act. Officers raised their glasses to the two heroes. In Pskov and in Kiev, people embraced in the streets. The rejoicing was such that in spite of Alexandra's heartbroken entreaties, Nicholas was unable to order the execution of the murderers. Educated opinion was virtually unanimous, though ordinary people were not so sure. One wounded soldier heard the news in hospital, and said: 'He was the first peasant to come close to the Tsar and Tsarina, and look what happened, the high-ups killed him.'

The New Year of 1917 was celebrated by the exiled socialist Lenin in Switzerland. In a lecture before a group of young Swiss

The return of the soldier. The German general Paul von Hindenburg marvelled at the scale of the enemy's casualties: 'In the great war ledger, the page on which the Russian losses were written has been torn out. No one knows the figures. Five or eight millions? We, too, have no idea. All we know is that sometimes in our battles with the Russians we had to remove the mounds of enemy corpses from before our trenches in order to get a clear field of fire against fresh assaulting waves. Imagination may try to reconstruct the figure of their losses, but an accurate calculation will remain forever a vain thing.'

The 'school' for Bolsheviks in Capri, Italy, run by Maxim Gorky. When Lenin (right) paid it a visit in 1908, he was living in Switzerland. His fellow émigré revolutionaries did not always impress him: 'The Geneva Bolsheviks are in a wretched state,' he wrote. 'Good lads all of them – but bloody useless at politics.'

workers in the Zurich Volkshaus a few weeks later, he said: 'We of the older generation may not live to see the decisive battles of this coming revolution.' So it was that the revolution of 1917 took all the politicians by surprise.

It was the women of Petrograd who took the first decisive steps on the road to revolution. That winter had been the coldest for many years. Fed up with queuing in the freezing winter streets, infuriated by the introduction of bread rationing, the women textile workers went on strike. Their menfolk followed. In all 90,000 workers went on strike that first morning. It was International Women's Day, 8 March by the Western calendar, or 23 February by the old-style Russian calendar.

The next day half the industrial workers in Petrograd were on strike. By the third day the number had risen to almost a quarter of a million.

The government did have contingency plans for dealing with insurrection, which relied on the troops of the Petrograd garrison. But here the government had made a fatal misjudgement.

MOCKOBCKOE OXPAHHOE OTДЪЛЕНIE. Ульяновъ Ленинъ Владимиръ

ABOVE *Lenin's mugshot from the files of the secret police in 1893. His friend Rosa Luxemburg declared: 'Look at the self-willed stubborn head. A real Russian peasant's head with a few faintly Asiatic lines. That man will try to overturn mountains. Perhaps he will be crushed by them. But he will never yield.'*

RIGHT *Leon Trotsky: with Lenin the most charismatic of the Bolshevik leaders. He took the boat home to Russia from New York in May 1917. Stalin was later one of the many who acknowledged Trotsky's pivotal role in the October coup: 'All the work of practical organization of the Revolution,' he wrote, 'the party owes principally and above all to Comrade Trotsky.'*

Yakov Sverdlov (BELOW LEFT), Nikolai Bukharin (BELOW RIGHT), Grigori Zinoviev (BELOW OPPOSITE LEFT), Lev Kamenev (BELOW OPPOSITE RIGHT): Four exiled Bolsheviks drawn back to Petrograd by the stirrings of revolution. All had to travel enormous distances: Sverdlov 2000 miles on horseback, Bukharin from New York, Kamenev on the famed sealed train with Lenin, and Zinoviev from imprisonment in Siberia.

The 26th was a Sunday, and the workers began to move towards the city centre. Petrograd was a city of great beauty, built on a network of islands criss-crossed by canals. The workers found the bridges closed to them, so they walked across the ice. Troops fired on them, killing forty, but they kept coming. It was to prove a turning point. Next morning, one by one, the military units began to mutiny. The Volynsky regiment refused orders to march out into the streets, shot their commanding officer and went over to the revolution. The workers were jubilant.

Alarmed at the news from his capital, Nicholas set off from the front to try to get home. Railway workers stopped his train at Pskov station, 170 miles from Petrograd. There, in a siding, he received the news of the mutiny of the Volynsky regiment by telegraph from General Khabalov, Chief of the Petrograd Military District. Khabalov reported that the whole city was in the hands of the revolutionaries, including the railway stations, telephone exchange and garrison artillery, and that all the government ministers had been arrested.

On the eighth day, the Tsar of all the Russias abdicated in his railway carriage on behalf of himself and his sick thirteen-year-old heir. 'To save Russia and keep the army at the front, I decided upon this step ... I left Pskov with heavy feelings; around me treason, cowardice, deceit,' he wrote.

It was the end of Romanov rule. In the bloody civil war still to come, almost nobody would raise the banner of the royal family. Its authority and its reputation had been squandered in the hopelessness of defeat.

Commoners and noblemen now joyfully took up the reins of power laid down by the Autocrat. At the Tauride Palace in Petrograd, a Provisional Government was put together by representatives of the old imperial parliament, the Duma. They were a fine collection of gentlemen who knew that in the long term their job was to sort out the peasant problem and introduce democratic elections to a proper parliament, the Constituent Assembly. In the short term, however, all agreed the task was clear. It was to meet their obligations to their allies and get the Russian armed forces back into the war.

There was a challenge right on the doorstep of the Provisional Government. In another wing of the same Tauride Palace, a rival political organization was setting up. It called itself the Soviet, or council, and was formed of deputies elected by soldiers and workers. Now all over Petrograd, and all over the country, soviets large and small were being elected in schools, factories, barracks and in the naval fortress of Kronstadt. They were a genuinely popular form of representative democracy.

The first thing the Petrograd Soviet did was to issue its Order Number One, which put elected committees in charge of army units, and demanded that officers be more polite to their men.

ABOVE *Street fighting days: the February Revolution, 1917.*

RIGHT *Alexander Kerensky (second from left) arrives at the imperial palace at Tsarskoye Selo near Petrograd. As Minister of Justice, his first job in the Provisional Government, he was responsible for the detention and safety of the Imperial Family.*

Though it was designed only to quiet the city garrison, news of this revolutionary measure soon spread throughout the land. Many soldiers and sailors interpreted Order Number One as a licence to go home. Even as the Provisional Government was promising to keep Russia in the war, the army was beginning to melt away.

The millions of 'peasants in uniform', illiterate, far from home, sullen and angry, were sick of floggings and wasted lives. Former infantry officer Vladimir Rukhadze, now ninety-four, describes the conditions. 'Eight of us ate out of one bowl,' he says. 'The parks displayed a notice: forbidden to dogs and soldiers.' As news of the revolution spread, fanned by clandestine propaganda from agitators at the front, the troops would simply creep away from the battlefield and go home. The soldiers' confidence was underlined by the first acts of the Provisional Government: it abolished the death penalty, even for military crimes, and dismantled the tsarist police.

The two organizations in the capital existed side by side throughout that long summer of 1917. They kept an uneasy distance from each other, but it was clear to intelligent observers where the real power lay. Guchkov, the Minister of War, remarked bitterly: 'The Provisional Government does not possess any real power, and its directives are carried out only to the extent that it is permitted by the Soviet of Workers' and Soldiers' Deputies, which enjoys all the essential elements of real power, since the troops, the railroads, the post and telegraph are all in its hands.'

While the two authorities danced around each other, the war continued. The Allies had welcomed the revolution in Russia, hoping it would haul the Russian military effort out of the doldrums. The enemy Germans, more sensible or more optimistic, could not believe their luck. They started offering free passage home to the most dangerous revolutionary exiles they could find, hoping to destabilize the situation still further. And that is how Lenin came to be put on a sealed train out of Germany, arriving at Petrograd's Finland Station in early April.

When Lenin came home to Russia he had been in exile for most of the previous seventeen years, running one wing of the small and quarrelsome Russian Social Democratic Party. His Bolsheviks were the radical left faction of this Marxist party, who had forced a split from the more conciliatory Mensheviks back in 1903. Lenin arrived to discover the Marxist intelligentsia arguing as usual about what should happen next. Their reading of the works of Karl Marx had made it clear that every society must go through the same stages of development: first feudalism, then capitalism, then socialism. Since Russia had never experienced capitalism, it had neither the wealth nor the massive working class necessary to effect a successful socialist revolution. So the

Marxists found themselves in the paradoxical position of welcoming the revolution as bourgeois, liberal and capitalist, and deferring the idea of socialism until some time in the future.

Lenin was to change all that. His train was welcomed at the Finland Station by a band playing 'La Marseillaise', because nobody had had time to learn the tune of the 'Internationale'. Cheering Bolshevik workers and sailors from the Baltic fleet lifted him on to an armoured car, where he gave a short speech. Let the workers take power now, he said. Let's end the war. His comrades were shocked. Only one other Bolshevik supported him: Alexandra Kollontai, the flamboyant, aristocratic feminist. His own party newspaper *Pravda* attacked him.

The compelling simplicity of his ideas would eventually attract thousands to the slogan: 'Peace! Bread! Land! And all power to the Soviets!' But it was to take Lenin seven months to persuade his comrades that his plans were not quite mad.

Meanwhile another political organization commanded the loyalty of most ordinary people. The Socialist Revolutionary Party had roots stretching back to the bomb-throwing nihilists of the nineteenth century. They were much more respectable now, but they still favoured taking the land from the landlords and giving it to the peasants. This was a wildly popular idea, and gave the SRs a majority on the Soviet and, as the summer wore on, a

A postcard of the First Provisional Government, one of a succession of administrations and coalitions which tried to ride the political storm between March and October 1917. Its members came from disparate backgrounds: Tereshchenko (top left) was a sugar magnate, Shingarev (top row second left) a doctor, Manuilov (bottom left) an economist, Guchkov (bottom centre) a Boer War veteran, and Nekrasov (bottom second right) a railway engineer. Although landowner Prince Lvov (top centre) was the government's nominal leader, Kerensky (top second right) was the dominant figure, thanks to his links with the Petrograd Soviet.

Kerensky (right), now War Minister, visits the front. His impassioned speeches urging the troops to fight on earned him the nickname 'Supreme Persuader-in-Chief'.

BELOW *May Day 1917. 'Between February and October,' wrote Kerensky of the continuing ferment, 'the revolution became a flood, and we could not halt or direct it.'*

commanding position in the Provisional Government. At first, one of their members, a young lawyer called Alexander Kerensky, had found himself the only socialist in a Cabinet dominated by liberals. This arrangement was dismissively described by Lenin as a case of ten capitalists and one hostage to democracy. But Kerensky was also deputy chairman of the Petrograd Soviet, and was soon to become Prime Minister. This ought to have made him unassailable.

The trouble was that Kerensky still believed in fighting the war. So in June he ordered a fresh offensive against Germany. It was a disaster: in three weeks, 60,000 more soldiers died. General Knox, head of the British Military Mission in Russia, concluded that the army was 'irretrievably ruined as a fighting organization'.

There was an explosion of popular anger at home. The streets filled again with furious demonstrators, war-weary soldiers, hungry families and citizens impatient for change. No date had yet been fixed for the long-awaited elections to the Constituent Assembly, thousands were unemployed due to factory closures, and the Bolsheviks were busy agitating. Banners began to appear on the streets: 'Peace! Bread! Land! All power to the Soviets!'

Kerensky's response to the July Days was swift. He clamped down on political freedom, and arrested so many Bolsheviks that Lenin had to shave off his beard and flee with false papers to Finland, where he spent the rest of the summer writing a book. And on 1 August, Kerensky appointed a new Supreme Commander-in-Chief, General Lavr Kornilov. Kornilov was appalled at the chaos and slack discipline he found on the battlefield and on the home front. He decided on the short sharp shock of a military coup, supported by the Muslim troops of his Savage Division from the mountains of the Caucasus. It didn't work. The Petrograd Soviet found a few Muslim troops of its own and sent them off to outface the counter-revolutionaries.

As the coup collapsed ignominiously, the stock of Kerensky's government fell perilously low. He sacked General Kornilov, but it was too late to prevent the wholesale collapse of support for the Social Revolutionaries. People said that all the party had managed to do during its term of office was put up tram fares.

Outside the cities, people were taking the law into their own hands, in agreement with the peasants of Samara, who said: 'The land must belong to those who work it with their hands, to those whose sweat flows.' Kornilov had already admitted that two million soldiers had now deserted the front. In all this chaos and incompetence, the Bolsheviks were the beneficiaries. In September they won their first outright majorities on the Petrograd and Moscow soviets, in yet another election. Lenin was delighted. He wrote to the Bolshevik Central Committee, urging them to prepare for insurrection, and threatened to resign as leader when nobody agreed with him.

LEFT *13,000 sailors from the Kronstadt naval base outside Petrograd arrive in the city at the end of August to help put down the attempted military coup led by General Lavr Kornilov, Commander-in-Chief of the Russian army.*

BELOW LEFT *Bolshevik tracts being distributed in the streets of Petrograd in August 1917.*

ABOVE *Officer cadets guard members of the Provisional Government in the Winter Palace, Petrograd, on the night – 25/26 October – that the Bolsheviks seized power. According to an old joke in the film business, more people were hurt during Eisenstein's restaging of the building being stormed for his epic* October *than during the actual event.*

RIGHT *The morning after in the Winter Palace. During the night, American journalist John Reed had witnessed wild scenes as crowds surged through the building: 'One man went strutting around with a bronze clock perched on his shoulder; another found a plume of ostrich feathers, which he stuck in his hat. The looting was just beginning when somebody cried, "Comrades! Don't take anything! This is the property of the People!" ... Many hands dragged the spoilers down.'*

ABOVE *Revolutionaries on the streets of Petrograd at the height of the October Revolution.*

BELOW *Bolshevik headquarters at the Smolny Institute, Petrograd. Smolny had been a smart girls' school, the Roedean of Russia. A massive building, 200 yards long, three storeys high and containing a hundred rooms, its corridors were so long that the Bolsheviks liked to joke that they needed bicycles to go from one office to another.*

Enthusiastic revolutionaries: sailors from the 'Aurora'. The cruiser is still preserved in Leningrad as a relic of the October coup d'état.

As autumn drew on, the atmosphere in the capital grew more and more charged. The city was full of deserters and street crime. The Tsar's palace at Tsarskoye Selo was pillaged. At the naval base of Kronstadt, brutal and unpopular officers were lynched by their men. Another new Commander-in-Chief, General Alexeyev, resigned on the grounds that there was no army left to lead. The fiery orator Leon Trotsky joined the Bolsheviks, was released from prison and elected as the head of the Petrograd Soviet.

By October the Bolsheviks were publishing twenty-five newspapers and had a membership approaching 40,000. And when delegates from soviets all over Russia arrived for a national congress, there was a clear majority for the Bolsheviks. The slogan 'All Power to the Soviets' was beginning to signify Bolshevik triumph.

Lenin arrived back from his hideaway in Finland determined to rally his reluctant party behind the clear public swing to the left. 'History will not forgive us if we do not take power now,' he said. At a clandestine meeting in a flat owned by the Menshevik Sukhanov (whose wife was a Bolshevik sympathizer), he finally got his way. The order for armed insurrection in favour of Soviet power was scribbled in a child's exercise book.

It was 25 October by the old Russian calendar, or 7 November by the Western style. In the small hours, groups of soldiers, sailors and workers, all Bolshevik supporters, began quietly occupying the railway stations, telephone exchanges and post office. The trams were still running, and the fashionable restaurants and theatres were still doing business. But at first light the State Bank was surrounded. A ring of troops surrounded the Winter Palace,

The Petrograd soviet. This council of soldiers and workers became the basis of the government after October.

where the Provisional Government had taken refuge.

The Congress of Soviets opened at 10.40 that night in the great white ballroom of the Smolny Institute, a former school for young ladies. As delegates argued furiously over the Bolshevik plan to take power in their name, insurrectionists were engaged in storming the Winter Palace.

All day small groups of soldiers and sailors had been getting inside and haranguing the confused officer cadets trying to guard the huge palace. By the evening, crowds were milling around the corridors. Eventually they found the room where the ministers, dignified to the last, were seated round their Cabinet table. 'In the name of the Military and Revolutionary Committee of the Petrograd Soviet, I declare the Provisional Government deposed!' cried the Bolshevik Vladimir Antonov-Ovseyenko. It was 2.10 in the morning of 26 October. They arrested all the ministers, but they did not catch Kerensky. He had fled to the front to rally resistance, travelling in an American embassy car.

That day Lenin went to the Congress, greeted by a tumult of cheering. He said simply: 'We shall now proceed to construct the socialist order.'

It had been a virtually bloodless coup, and it was over very quickly. Afterwards, Trotsky admitted that it had all been a bit of an anticlimax. 'The final act of the revolution seems, after all this, too brief, too dry, too businesslike ...'

The new government was called the Council of People's Commissars. Lenin thought the word 'Commissar' had a fine revolutionary ring.

There was one Bolshevik for every six hundred Russians.

Leaders of the Revolution. In this contemporary photomontage Lenin and Trotsky take pride of place. Stalin is not included.

RIGHT *The upper classes are put to work. Snow in the streets was one Moscow tradition unaffected by the Revolution.*

The Imperial Family in captivity. When the October Revolution took place, they were being held in Tobolsk, Siberia.

RIGHT *The end of the old empire: the head of a statue of Tsar Alexander III, father of Nicholas II, bites the Moscow dust.*

2 Winners and Losers

In November 1918 the Bolsheviks celebrated the first anniversary of their revolution. They unveiled a statue of Marx and Engels outside the Bolshoi Theatre in Moscow, and Lenin led the mass singing of revolutionary songs. They had given themselves a new name: the All-Russian Communist Party. They had nationalized the factories, given land to the peasants, legalized divorce and modernized the archaic Russian calendar and alphabet. And their leader had survived an assassination attempt.

But the party which offered itself as the first domino of an international proletarian revolution was still perilously alone in the world. Abroad, workers' revolt seemed as far away as ever. At home, the first socialist state was to be challenged by no fewer than nineteen opposition governments. And Lenin, the man who had pledged to bring peace to a war-torn nation, was now calling for three million Red soldiers to fight a bloody civil war.

The October Revolution had swept the Bolsheviks to power on their promise to end the slaughter of the Great War. Their first act had been to order General Dukhonin, Commander-in-Chief of the Russian Army, to sue for peace. When he refused, they sent a new commander along with a band of Kronstadt sailors. Dukhonin was lynched.

Separately, and in disguise, Generals Kornilov and Denikin made their way south. They arrived in the Cossack capital of Novocherkassk, on the river Don, and began to try to raise money and to assemble a volunteer White Army of resistance to the Red coup.

The first Red commander sent against them was Antonov-Ovseyenko, the man who had arrested the Provisional Government during the storming of the Winter Palace. All he had was a force of inexperienced volunteers drawn from the Red Guards, a working-class factory militia who elected their own officers. They fought from railway trains which steamed up and down the lines.

Those first skirmishes were played out against the background of further controversial actions by the Bolsheviks. A week after the coup d'état, elections had finally been held to the democratic Constituent Assembly. The Bolsheviks had won only a quarter of the seats to this new parliament, and when the delegates assembled in January 1918, Red Guards closed the

ABOVE *Sailors who helped to dissolve the democratically-elected Constituent Assembly in January 1918. Lenin defended the abrupt closure thus: 'Not a single problem of the class struggle has been resolved during the course of history except by force. If force proceeds from the exploited working masses and against the exploiters – yes, then we are in favour of force. Therefore, comrades, to all complaints and accusations that we practise terror, dictatorship, civil war, we will reply – yes, we have openly declared what no other government has ever been able to declare – yes, we have started the war against the exploiters.'*

BELOW *The Bolsheviks met formidable obstacles to the spread of revolution. Red Guards briefly seized power in the Crimea in January 1918, but Soviet rule was only secured there by force of arms three years later.*

A regiment of Cossacks in the First World War. This elite professional fighting force had its origins in the seventeenth century, when bands of runaway serfs and other exiles began to congregate on the eastern and southern borders of the Russian empire. They formed their own proud and democratic societies, and were brought into service by the Tsars to secure Russia's borders against the Mongols.

session, evacuated the hall and barred the doors. Russia's long-awaited parliament had lasted just one day.

Two hundred shock units of Baltic sailors were sent into the provinces to help confirm Soviet power. A decree ordered the arrest of leading members of the liberal Kadet party as 'enemies of the people'. Freedom of the press was severely restricted.

In the capital there was continuing resistance. The government had no cash because all the bank clerks went on strike. Lenin telegraphed Stockholm: 'Urgently find and send here three highly skilled accountants to work on reform of the banks.'

Civil servants refused to work with their new masters. Trotsky, newly appointed Commissar for Foreign Affairs, could only get into his ministry building with the help of a band of armed sailors. The first thing he did there was to carry out the Bolshevik promise to end the war with Germany.

The armistice was negotiated among the ruins of Brest-Litovsk, a town behind German lines in occupied Poland which today is in Soviet Belorussia. The German peace conditions demanded huge and humiliating losses of territory, including the Ukraine, in the heartland of the old Russian Empire. But Lenin told the Petrograd Soviet: 'To carry on a revolutionary war, an army is necessary, and we do not have one. It is a question of signing the terms now, or of signing the death sentence of the Soviet government three weeks later.' There were cries of 'traitor' and 'German spy', but he won the argument.

Trotsky relinquished his job in foreign affairs and became

Checking papers in German-occupied Kiev. After Brest-Litovsk, Germany controlled the Ukraine until the end of World War I, in November 1918. A short-lived Ukrainian nationalist government succumbed to Soviet power in 1920.

The map shows:

The Eastern front on 7 November, 1917

Occupied by German troops in March 1918, as a result of the treaty of Brest-Litovsk

0 — Miles — 300

0 — Kilometres — 400

FINLAND · Lake Ladoga · Helsinki · Petrograd · SWEDEN · Baltic Sea · Pskov · Riga · MOSCOW · Vilna · Smolensk · GERMANY · POLAND · R U S S I A · Warsaw · Voronezh · Brest-Litovsk · Kiev · Kharkov · Poltava · Novocherkassk · AUSTRIA-HUNGARY · Odessa · Simferopol · ROMANIA · Black Sea · BULGARIA · Batum · TURKEY

Under the Treaty of Brest-Litovsk, the Bolsheviks paid a high price for peace with Germany, losing more than one and quarter million square miles of territory.

Commissar for War. His task: to create a Workers' and Peasants' Red Army. The original idea was to defend the revolution against external enemies, like the Germans, who now occupied the Ukraine. For that reason many non-Bolshevik patriotic military professionals wanted to help. In two years almost 50,000 former officers of the Tsar were taken into the Red Army.

There were huge arguments in the Party about the role of these 'bourgeois experts'. Finally it was agreed to appoint reliable political commissars to keep the military men in line. Trotsky called this the 'iron corset'.

In the course of the next three years, Trotsky's army was to grow to five million men, commanded from his personal armoured train. His mobile headquarters covered 65,000 miles. It had a radio, a map room, a printing press, secretarial staff, a Rolls-Royce, ammunition, medicine, and a platoon dressed all in leathers. Trotsky ran a competition to design a new uniform, which produced the distinctive pointed hat. He travelled the fronts whipping up morale and imposing ferocious discipline, promising to shoot the political commissar and military commander of any unit which retreated without orders. When one unit from Petrograd hijacked a steamer, he sent a gunboat after them and the death sentence was passed over commissar, commander and every tenth man.

The civil war which engulfed the Russian Empire began properly in the early summer of 1918, when the new government unexpectedly lost control of half the railways in the country – to a foreign legion. Thousands of Czech nationals had been working in Russia when war broke out, and had formed their own legion to fight on the Allied side. Now they were 40,000 professional soldiers, trying to get home eastwards by way of the Trans-Siberian railway.

A small incident in May in the Urals town of Chelyabinsk set them off. The local soviet arrested a group of Czech soldiers after a brawl with a trainload of Hungarian prisoners of war. Within three months the Czechs controlled the entire Trans-Siberian, and with it, two-thirds of the land area of all Russia. Their successes brought them within striking distance of another Urals town: Ekaterinburg. Here the Tsar and his family were kept under house arrest. They had been imprisoned for more than a year. Nobody knew what to do with them.

What really happened is still a matter of controversy. The Czechs were on the outskirts of the city. The imperial family would be a great prize to any captors. It is generally accepted that on 17 July 1918, local Bolsheviks, with or without orders from Lenin in Moscow, shot the Tsar, his wife and their five children and concealed the bodies.

The Germans used public hangings to reinforce their rule in the Ukraine.

Is this the skull of Tsar Nicholas II? In 1989, Soviet writer Geli Ryabov published this photograph to back up a claim that he had solved the mystery of the Imperial Family's fate. He said that he had found their grave outside Ekaterinburg (now Sverdlovsk). The bodies of the Tsar, the Tsarina and their five children had been hurriedly buried after a truck driven by their executioners became stuck in a swamp.

ABOVE *Fanya Kaplan, Lenin's would-be assassin. Before her execution she explained, 'I have long had the intention of killing Lenin. In my eyes he has betrayed the Revolution. I was for the Constituent Assembly and I still am.'*

BELOW *Lenin at the Kremlin 'photocall' staged by his friend Vladimir Bonch-Bruevich (right) to prove his recovery from Kaplan's bullets, which had penetrated his neck and lungs.*

This brutality towards the imperial family was part of a pattern of internal repression which was becoming fiercer under the impact of civil war. The final straw came six weeks later, when more gunshots rang out. Lenin had been shot in the chest, arm and neck by a young Social Revolutionary, Fanya Kaplan.

Fanya Kaplan was executed. Lenin was filmed some months later, to prove he had recovered from the assassination attempt. But his health never really rallied. The Bolshevik response was the promulgation of an official state of Red Terror, directed by the leather-jacketed secret policemen of the Special Commission or Cheka, forerunner of today's KGB. Thousands were executed and many more imprisoned in the concentration camps which made their first appearance that autumn of 1918.

The two pretexts for the Terror, the Czech legion and the Socialist Revolutionary Party, joined up in Samara on the Volga, claiming to rule in the name of the Constituent Assembly. Theirs was just one of nineteen alternative governments to appear during the course of the war. Most were incompetent and irrelevant. But, round the edges of the old empire, governments sprang up which bore the hopes of millions for national self-determination.

On the far side of the Caucasus mountains to the south lay a trio of small nations, historically sandwiched between the powerful empires of Russia and the Ottoman Turks. Azerbaijan was a Turkish and Muslim land, Armenia its Christian neighbour. The third was the ancient kingdom of Kartli-Kakheti, or Georgia, where people had lived for fifty thousand years. Its small population was economically backward, but culturally rich and proud, and its capital city Tbilisi had produced a thriving national liberation movement.

On 26 May 1918, Georgian and red flags were raised together over the palace of the former Russian Imperial Viceroy. Georgia was declared independent.

The new Georgia was governed by a left-wing coalition headed by Mensheviks, Marxists who objected to the Bolshevik coup and hoped to keep Georgia out of the Russian civil war. Their honeymoon of independence was to last only so long as the Red Army remained preoccupied with war with the Whites.

For a while the Whites looked such a formidable enemy that there was even a futures market in landowners' estates, gambling on their victory. At the Versailles peace conference, the victorious Allies gave limited recognition to the Siberian government headed by the White Admiral Kolchak.

His regime was plagued by corruption, bribery and inefficiency, and his military effort wasted over the vast distances from his Siberian headquarters. But the Whites did have one advantage: the support of foreign troops. The British had been involved in the war virtually since the beginning, in an attempt to keep the Russians in the war against Germany. Even after the German

One of the first Red Army detachments marches through Red
Square soon after the launch of Trotsky's recruiting drive
in April 1918. In the early days, military know-how was
provided by former tsarist officers.

Czechs on the Trans-Siberian Railway in May 1918. Their
seizure of Russia's main transport artery led Trotsky to
order: 'Every armed Czechoslovak found on the railway is
to be shot on the spot.'

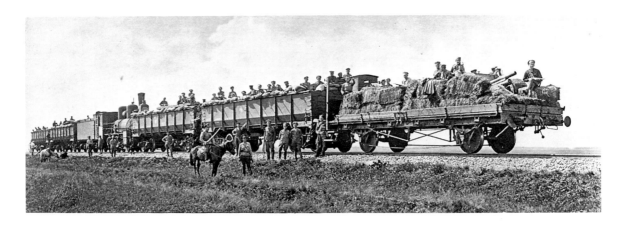

defeat, they stayed on to fight the Bolsheviks; Churchill said: 'Having defeated all the tigers and lions, I don't like to be defeated by baboons.' British ships surrounded ports to the north in Archangelsk, to the south in the Crimea, and to the far east at Vladivostok. There were Americans and French too.

The Bolsheviks were furious at this interference in their affairs, and made full use of the issue of Western imperialism in propaganda designed to appeal to Russian patriotism. But no Western power ever sent troops to the front line of the Russian civil war. What they did contribute to the White cause, as long as it remained fashionable, was millions of pounds' worth of aeroplanes, tanks, machine guns, uniforms and training. This cut both ways, given the confusion and racketeering of the times. The British officer Captain Francis McCullagh wrote: 'The uniforms walked over to the Reds, thousands at a time, with the Whites inside them.'

Though at the top the war was fought between implacably opposed ideologies, in the ranks men joined up, as always, because they were hungry or because they had no choice. Desertion and typhus were endemic. Repeated mobilizations and conscription were the ways both sides filled their armies. As areas changed hands or prisoners were taken, men went over from Red to White and back again. Whole units changed sides, shot their officers, deserted and went home.

The Czech Legion enters Irkutsk, an important bridgehead on its way to capturing the whole of the Trans-Siberian Railway.

LEFT *Foreign powers intervene in the Civil War: Czech, American, British and Japanese troops in Vladivostok in the Far East.*

RIGHT *Semyon Budyonny, one of the Civil War's most colourful characters and commander of the Reds' shock troops, the First Cavalry Army.*

ABOVE *A dreadnought of the 'Train War'. Immediately after October, revolutionaries took to Russia's vast railway system to fight opposition in outlying regions of the empire.*

LEFT *British sailors on the Arctic Murmansk front after a skirmish with the Reds.*

Officers under the command of White General Alexander Kolchak examine the spoils of war.

On all sides, it was a cruel and desperate war. In terms of military atrocities, there was little to choose between the Red Terror and the White Terror. At Stavropol, the 'black Baron' Wrangel captured 3000 Bolsheviks and shot more than 300 officers and NCOs to encourage their men to defect. At Kharkov, Bolsheviks nailed epaulettes to White shoulders while the victims were still alive. All sides were guilty of pogroms against civilians, especially Jews.

The confusion was a great comfort to a third force. The Greens were local freebooters – Cossack, peasant or nationalist – and they fought anyone, Red or White. Most swashbuckling among them was the Ukrainian anarchist partisan Nestor Makhno. He divided his booty with local peasants, which made him very popular. He even set up a short-lived anarchist republic. Its black-flagged army was dedicated to two goals: 'extermination of the rich bourgeoisie and of the Bolshevik commissars who use force to uphold a bourgeois social order'.

And while Red commissars, White officers and Green partisans fought for honour and glory and their own idea of love for the motherland, the peasant masses suffered and endured and waited for it all to blow over. Confused peasant insurgents on the Volga rose under banners proclaiming: 'Long live the Bolsheviks, down with the Communists.' Roads were blocked by refugees. Kiev changed hands sixteen times. The Reds would come and commandeer the cathedral for grain storage; the Whites would come and hold a Te Deum in it. Several different currencies circulated.

By the late autumn of 1919 the White threat looked fatal, as General Denikin's forces raced towards Moscow and the heart of the Soviet republic. But this was an illusion. Between mid-November and the beginning of January 1920, the overstretched Whites collapsed. They retreated in disorder for 450 miles, beyond the river Don, to their last stand.

Always fighting from the periphery, the small White armies were strung out over impossible distances. The men were supposed to feed themselves, which often simply meant vicious looting from the peasants. Wrangel admitted that the Volunteer Army retreated 'through places where the population had learned to hate it'. And Trotsky called Mamontov's band of nine thousand Don Cossacks 'a comet with a filthy tail of robbery and rape'.

But Mamontov and his mounted warriors had taught Trotsky one crucial lesson. The result was the First Cavalry Army, the legendary Konarmia. It was formed in November 1919 under Semyon Budyonny, who had been a sergeant in the Tsar's cavalry, and its recruiting slogan was: 'Proletarians, to horse!' Horses were out of fashion among military theorists, but the Konarmia was astonishingly successful. They were so fast and so good at destroying communications that the first their enemy knew of them was the sound of their hooves.

Felix Dzerzhinsky, founder of the Cheka, the Bolshevik secret police. It admitted executing 12,733 people between 1918 and 1921. Dzerzhinsky said, 'The Cheka must defend the revolution and conquer the enemy, even if the sword falls occasionally on the heads of the innocent.'

RIGHT *Trotsky and the Red Army. He believed his personal armoured train was the key to the transformation of amateur Red Guards into proper soldiers: '. . . the flabby, panicky mob would be transformed in two or three weeks into an efficient fighting force. What was needed for this? At once much and little. It needed good commanders, a few dozen experienced fighters, a dozen or so of Communists ready to make any sacrifice, boots for the barefooted, a bath-house, an energetic propaganda campaign, food, underwear, tobacco and matches. The train took care of all this.'*

Товарищ Троцкій

Early in 1920, everything fell apart for the Whites. The Reds appointed their finest young professional as Commander-in-Chief in the Caucasus, the flamboyant twenty-six-year-old Mikhail Tukhachevsky. Handsome and ambitious, he was determined to be dead or famous by the age of thirty. White morale collapsed as Odessa fell in the south, Archangelsk in the north, and Kolchak's regime in the east. The Allies decided their intervention had cost too much money, and the sea blockade was lifted. General Denikin's staff lost control. His troops fled past hungry refugees and marauding Greens, south towards the sea and the hope of evacuation.

In the Black Sea port of Odessa, many were killed as British naval officers enforced the rule of women and children first. In Novorossisk, thousands of White families and troops struggled through mountain passes in biting weather towards the port and the waiting Royal Navy. At the waterside fleeing Cossacks shot their horses, and starving refugees took them for food. The Red artillery shelled the port, and many who were left behind drowned trying to swim to the ships.

General Denikin went to his exile aboard a British destroyer. He would never see Russia again. Later he wrote: 'When we put to sea it was already night. Only bright lights scattered in the thick darkness marked the coast of the receding Russian land. They grow dimmer and vanish. Rossiya, my Motherland...'

At the same time, at the other end of the empire, Kolchak was shot by Bolsheviks. There was only one White general left: Baron Wrangel.

Mikhail Tukhachevsky, a former tsarist officer. The Civil War launched his brilliant career in the Red Army.

This photograph of a group of White generals was published in the West after 'being smuggled past Bolsheviks in a box of insect powder'. General Anton Denikin (third left, front row) was Commander-in-Chief in South Russia. He said, 'My programme consists of restoring Russia and then raising cabbages.'

The Konarmia. Founded in response
to the successes of White mounted
detachments, the Red Cavalry had
15,000 men under arms.

BELOW *Nestor Makhno, the Ukrainian anarchist. A thorn in the flesh of both
Reds and Whites.*

ABOVE *Survivors: Red troops after a skirmish. Total Civil War casualties are unknown. At least 800,000 soldiers are thought to have died, more than half from epidemics of disease which ravaged the battle zones.*

LEFT *Japanese troops with the bodies of Bolsheviks. Bitterness about the intervention of foreign troops persists to this day in the USSR.*

*The end of the Civil War.
Baron Wrangel, the last
White commander, sails into
exile aboard the cruiser*
General Kornilov *in
November 1920.*

Following the panic evacuations from the Crimea, in April 1920 Wrangel had begun to form the last White Army. But he had a quarter of a million people to feed, and he knew he was outnumbered by three to one. He began to plan a final evacuation.

The autumn of 1920 was the coldest for years in the Crimea. The White infantry, tired and freezing, had to stuff their shirts with moss. On 7 November, the third anniversary of the Bolshevik revolution, it was fifteen degrees below zero. And that was the night the Reds attacked.

Seventy years later, Isaak Mints, the last surviving political commissar of the Cavalry Army, can still remember the battle to gain control of the slender Perekop Isthmus, which marks off the Crimean peninsula. 'We had three lines of defences to get past: a barbed-wire barricade, the eighteenth-century Turkish wall, and then trenches. But we had a stroke of luck. Freak winds froze the mud flats beside the isthmus, so we could pick our way around,' he recalls.

Wrangel ordered that every seaworthy boat in the Crimean ports should be commandeered. And four days after the Red attack he issued the command: 'I now order the evacuation and embarkation at the Crimean ports of all those who are following the Russian army on its road to Calvary ... may God grant us strength and wisdom to endure this period of Russian misery and to survive it.'

One hundred and twenty-six ships, carrying 145,693 men, women and children, set off for Constantinople.

Wrangel spoke to his remaining cadets on the quay. 'We are going into exile: we are not going as beggars with outstretched hands, but with our heads held high, conscious of having done our duty to the end.'

Denikin died peacefully in the USA in 1947. Wrangel died in Brussels in 1928, after setting up the world organization of Russian war veterans. The anarchist Makhno died in his bed in poverty in Paris in 1935.

The rout of the Whites could not be celebrated for long, however. The year 1921 opened with a long list of problems for Lenin and his government. The economy was ruined. Inflation was astronomical, and all wages were paid in kind. Hundreds of thousands of workers had given up city life and gone home to the country. The left-wing oppositionist Alexander Shlyapnikov ironically congratulated Lenin on being 'in the vanguard of a non-existent class'.

The village economy had collapsed into a state of nineteenth-century backwardness. What the peasants could grow was forcibly requisitioned by 'iron detachments' of Bolsheviks to feed the hungry cities. Thousands of orphaned children roamed the streets, thieving and robbing, prey to disease and cruelty. The final blow was a terrible famine which struck the whole Volga region. The Americans sent aid. Even so, millions starved to death.

Once the peasants realized that their hated landlords had gone for good, they began to fight back against Red requisitioning and the Bolshevik dictatorship of the proletariat. Unorganized, armed only with pitchforks, scythes and flails, hungry and angry peasants rose up against their new oppressors.

The revolt was strongest around Tambov, in the fertile black earth region three hundred miles south of Moscow. Lenin gave Antonov-Ovseyenko the new job title of Commisssar for Repression, and sent him south to sort the trouble out. The Commissar reported in January 1921 that half the peasantry was starving. People ate acorns, weeds and chaff.

A provincial peasant congress had already called for the over-throw of the Communist regime which had brought the country to misery, ruin and shame. But the firepower of the peasant rebellion was centred on a group of desperate Greens. Their leader was a mysterious and romantic figure called Antonov, who had used his former position as chief of police to amass a cache of arms and to gather support for a bloody campaign of terrorism against the Communists.

His motley band of 20,000 untrained fighters committed arson and pulled up railway lines. If they got their hands on Young Communist or Cheka officials, they would bury their victims alive, crucify them, flay them or set wild dogs on them. Lenin admitted: 'We are barely hanging on.'

But in the end, the fighting peasants of Tambov could prove no match for 50,000 Red troops, who reimposed Soviet power by force. People were shot summarily in batches, and entire villages exiled. The military leader of the operation was, once again, Tukhachevsky.

The glamorous young Red commander was fresh from putting down an insurrection at the heart of the Bolshevik fortress. The rebellion in Tambov, and a new wave of strikes in Petrograd, had struck a chord of sympathy among the sailors of the Baltic Fleet stationed at the Kronstadt island naval base, only seventeen miles from the northern capital in the Gulf of Finland. This traditional bastion of Communist support mutinied. The sailors' demands included immediate re-election of the soviets by free and secret ballot, freedom of speech and association, full rights for the peasants and an end to the special privileges of the Communist Party.

As the Tenth Party Congress met, Tukhachevsky mobilized soldiers and party cadres under Trotsky's leadership. It was spring, and the ice which separated the island fortress from the mainland was beginning to crack. As the Red forces advanced across the frozen water, they watched helplessly as comrades fell through the melting ice. In bloody hand-to-hand fighting the

Famine on the Volga, 1921.
American industrialist Dr
Armand Hammer saw
'children with their limbs
shrivelled to the size of sticks
and their bellies horribly
bloated by eating grass and
herbs, which they were unable
to digest ... begging piteously
for bread – for life itself – in
a dreadful ceaseless whine.'

'The carrion crows and
vagrant dogs fared well in
those dreadful days,' wrote
Hammer.

Red soldiers managed to put down a revolt by Red sailors. It was a traumatic turning point in the Party's history.

At the Party Congress, delegates were bewildered and angry. To this day, the men who took part in the assault on Kronstadt claim the sailors were swine who wanted counter-revolution. And it was fear of counter-revolution which led the Congress to pass two crucial decisions.

First, they dealt with the threat of economic collapse by abolishing the forced requisition of food from the peasants. They

introduced a tax in kind instead, together with a certain amount of free trade. This New Economic Policy was the *perestroika* of its day. Lenin only got it through the Party by once again threatening to resign.

Second, they clamped down on discipline within the Party. All the small factions of vociferous critics of the party line were told to shut up or face expulsion. Opposition was outlawed. Economic relaxation was accompanied by fierce political tightening. In the absence of any international revolutions, an age of new realism had dawned. The Party was determined to survive, and that meant protecting itself and its borders by all means available.

So Caucasian dreams of independence also collapsed, one by one, as the defeat of the Whites led the Red Army to turn its attention to the south. The Red Army met no armed resistance as it forced the retirement of the Muslim nationalist Musavat government in Baku, and declared a Soviet republic of Azerbaijan. Armenia succumbed too. And in February 1921, the 11th Red Army crossed the border into Georgia, bringing Soviet power on the points of their bayonets. The Menshevik government sailed away to exile in Paris.

Melting into the background. Before crossing the ice to storm the Kronstadt naval base, where the sailors were in revolt against the Red government, Tukhachevsky's troops camouflaged themselves by wearing white sheets over their uniforms.

A Leninist curiosity. One of the nine Rolls Royce cars ordered for Lenin at the 1920 London Motor Show. This one was 'winterized' at the Putilov Works in Petrograd.

BELOW *Electric light comes to the village of Botino, near Moscow. 'Electrification is to my mind the most momentous of the great tasks that confront us,' said Lenin. He saw it as the key to the modernization of Russia's economy.*

RIGHT *'Communism is Soviet power plus the electrification of the whole country.' With this slogan Lenin launched his campaign to bring electricity to all of the Soviet Union within ten years.*

The Bolsheviks had appointed the Georgian revolutionary Joseph Stalin as Commissar of Nationalities, and it fell to him to work out government policy towards national minorities. The Bolsheviks had always claimed they were in favour of national self-determination. But Stalin was not alone in putting the interests of proletarian revolution before what he called 'bourgeois nationalism'.

Lenin, who was already ill after the first of the strokes which were to kill him, launched his own investigation into the methods of the Commissar of Nationalities when the Georgian Bolshevik Central Committee resigned en masse. Appalled by the crude political bullying he found, he wrote to Trotsky imploring him to help sort it out. So it was that in December 1923, in his last few weeks of life, semi-paralysed and very sick, with Stalin already General Secretary, the old leader embarked on a struggle to

The leadership: Lenin (left), Trotsky (right) and Mikhail Kalinin, the Head of State.

Stalin's first impressions on meeting Lenin in 1905: 'I had hoped to see the mountain eagle of our party, the great man, great physically as well as politically ... How great was my disappointment to see a most ordinary-looking man.'

Some of Lenin's last thoughts on Stalin in his 1923 'Testament': 'Comrade Stalin, having become Secretary-General, has unlimited authority concentrated in his hands, and I am not sure whether he will always be capable of using that authority with sufficient caution.'

contain the already burgeoning bureaucratic power. It was, of course, too late.

The old leader died after his third stroke on 21 January 1924. His death stunned his comrades. Factory sirens blared out to call people to hear the news. Thousands lined the snowy streets as the genius of the revolution was borne on his final journey.

Plans were made to build Lenin a mausoleum equal to his reputation, and an Immortalization Commission was set up to organize it. Petrograd was renamed Leningrad. It was suggested that Sunday should be renamed Leninday. His face appeared on cigarette packets, and inkwells in the shape of the mausoleum became popular. The trade in Lenin curios grew so swiftly that the Immortalization Commission banned anything it had not licensed. The tomb of Tutankhamun had recently been discovered in Egypt, and this led to the decision that the corpse should be embalmed. So, to the horror of his widow, the old atheist's remains became the centre of a semi-religious cult.

'To us all is permitted,' he wrote, 'for we are the first in the world to raise the sword not in the name of enslaving and oppressing anyone, but in the name of freeing all from bondage ...'

Lenin and his wife Krupskaya. He had proposed to her in 1897 in a letter written in invisible ink. After Lenin's death, Stalin is said to have remarked that if Krupskaya did not stop criticizing him, the Party would have to find Lenin another widow.

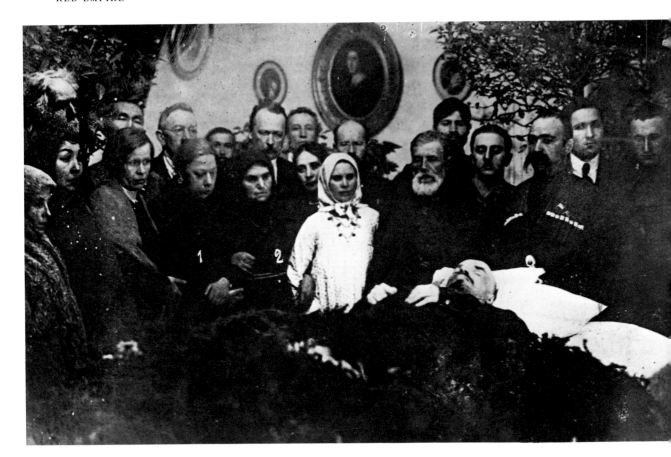

LEFT *Lenin's body lies in state at his country house at Gorki, near Moscow, in January 1924. Krupskaya (front row fourth left) and Lenin's sister (beside Krupskaya) are among the mourners.*

BELOW LEFT *The people of Moscow queue to pay their last respects at the lying-in-state at the old Nobles' Club. Bonch-Bruevich described the scene inside:*

'Everyone stood in silence and looked into the placid, pallid face of one who had always been very dear and close to them, and bent their heads in a single motion as if obeying an inner voice. There was silence. Oh, how quiet it grew, here where so recently a heart full of fire and passion had beaten.'

ABOVE *27 January 1924. Lenin's coffin is carried to Red Square by members of the Central Committee. Left to right: Stalin, Kamenev, Sapronov, Rudzutak, Molotov, Kalinin and Bukharin.*

BELOW *The scene at the mausoleum in Red Square. The writer Nadezhda Mandelstam described Lenin's funeral as 'like the funeral of a tsar of Muscovy'.*

3 Class Warriors

The great white passenger ships lined up against the quay at Moscow's River Station form a romantic vision of past glories. The *Alexander Nevsky* and the *Fyodor Dostoevsky* still cruise gently south towards Astrakhan and the Caspian Sea. They pass the massive cranes of the commercial docks, rise through giant locks hidden among the trees and flats of suburban Moscow, and leave the Moscow river by ship canal to steam for miles through the peaceful countryside of forest and lakes towards the river Volga.

Many of the men and women who dug the mud and laid the stones did not live to sail down the engineering miracle they created. For the Moscow–Volga Canal is a reminder of human cruelty and a testament to human endurance. It was dug by hand by thousands of slaves during four years of deadly labour: just one of the massive engineering projects forced into life by Russia's new leader, Joseph Stalin.

When the members of the Central Committee shared the burden of carrying Lenin's coffin in 1924, few of them knew that he had dictated a last testament giving his views on the suitability of his colleagues to succeed him. He had barely a good word to

The secret policeman's funeral. When Felix Dzerzhinsky died in 1926, Stalin was emerging victorious from the struggle to succeed Lenin. Soon all the pall-bearers were to fall victim to Stalin's ruthless pursuit of absolute power. Rykov (left), Yagoda (in cap) and Kamenev (fifth from left) were all shot, Trotsky (fourth from left) assassinated, Rakovsky (behind Stalin's shoulder) imprisoned and exiled. Even Kalinin (third left), though Head of State, saw his wife sent to the Gulag.

say about any of them. Trotsky was able but too self-confident, and Bukharin was not a proper Marxist. But Lenin's fiercest condemnation was reserved for Stalin, General Secretary for the past three years.

'Stalin is too rude,' he said, 'and this fault, quite tolerable in our midst or in relations among Communists, becomes intolerable for one who holds the office of General Secretary. Therefore I propose to the comrades that they consider a means of removing Stalin from the post and appointing to it another person ... more patient, more loyal, more polite and more considerate to comrades, less capricious and so forth.'

Lenin's widow, Nadezhda Krupskaya, forwarded the document to the Central Committee. Stalin offered to resign, but his comrades rejected the idea. Within a few years most of those who had kept a copy were to be shot for 'being in possession of a counter-revolutionary document, the so-called Testament of Lenin'.

During Lenin's last illness, Stalin was already the most powerful man in the Party. He was the man who knew everything that went on, from the top echelons down to the newest cadres. His nickname was Comrade Card-Index.

The opposition to his rise to supreme power was astonishingly ineffectual. Afraid for their isolated and ramshackle new society, and committed to the party they believed was the only hope for the future, many loyal Communists buried their worries about the lack of democracy in the Party until it was too late. Even Trotsky showed an almost bashful unwillingness to save himself. 'My party – right or wrong,' he said. 'I know one cannot be right

Leon Trotsky (left) in exile. But Stalin kept an eye on his arch-enemy. Unknown to Trotsky, the man on the right was a secret agent working for Stalin.

against the Party ... for history has not created other ways for the realization of what is right.' It was a statement millions would come to regret.

It was not cowardice that held these fearless old revolutionaries back. Their whole philosophy had been based on the sacrifice of political freedom for party unity.

This controversial principle had always been one of the main differences marking out the Bolsheviks from the mainstream of pre-revolutionary Russian socialism. Lenin argued forcibly that a socialist party should welcome only professional revolutionaries, confident of leading the proletariat from the front. This idea of the vanguard party sounded dangerously elitist to many, and Lenin's ideas were rejected by most socialists of the time as authoritarian. But as an organizational tool, uniting carefully selected and dedicated members, the Leninist party offered an unrivalled source of political strength. All the old Bolsheviks supported it. And this was the background which allowed Stalin to consolidate his power.

The party from which Trotsky was to be purged was by now a very different organization to the tightly knit group of militants which had forged the October Revolution. Already in 1921 *Pravda*'s columns had thundered: 'A situation is gradually taking shape in which one can "rise in the world", make a career for oneself, get a bit of power, only by entering the service of the Soviet regime.' So Stalin did not invent the bureaucratic machine which he ran from Moscow. But hundreds of thousands of new members owed their allegiance and their promotion to him and to the secretariat. They gave him an unassailable power base.

For a while after Lenin's death, Stalin shared power with two powerful big city Party bosses: Grigory Zinoviev from Leningrad and Lev Kamenev from Moscow. Their alliance lasted for as long as it took to squeeze Trotsky out of the succession, at which point Stalin turned against his partners and took sole charge of the reins of power which Lenin had tried to deny him.

On 7 November 1927, the tenth anniversary of the revolution, Trotsky called a demonstration of protest at Stalin's policies in Moscow. It was broken up by the secret policemen of the OGPU. A foreign correspondent observed that he would 'never forget the bitterness written on Trotsky's face after hours of such futile effort'. Within a month the hero of the Red Army was dragged kicking and screaming from his flat by OGPU agents, who put him on a train and sent him to far-off Kazakhstan. It was the beginning of a lifelong exile for the rival Stalin had dismissed years before as 'pretty but useless'.

As Stalin surveyed the state of the country and the party over which he now held sway, he was becoming convinced that precious time had been wasted in fruitless daydreams. What was needed was action to shore up the defences of the tottering empire,

Rykov (left) and Stalin (right) voting at the 15th Party Congress in 1927. They passed a resolution demanding that 'the task of uniting and transforming the small individual peasant holdings into large collectives must become the principal task of the Party in the villages'.

and to haul the USSR into the ranks of the world powers. He formally abandoned the old dream of world revolution, and proclaimed his plan to build socialism in one country.

'We are fifty or a hundred years behind the advanced countries,' he said. 'We must catch up this distance in ten years. Either we do it or we go under.'

So in 1928 a second Communist revolution was unleashed. This was revolution from above. Cruel and daring, it swept away millions of lives and transformed the Soviet Union beyond recognition.

Among the first things to be jettisoned were more of the cherished ideals of Russian socialism. Stalin condemned the goal of equality in wages as a 'petty bourgeois prejudice'. He introduced the 'party envelopes' which enclosed big perks for loyal members. He abandoned any notion of workers' control, and declared that factories were to be run on the principle of one-man management. His lieutenant Lazar Kaganovich said the factory should quake when the director walked through.

The First Five-Year Plan, presented to the Party in 1928, laid down targets for the production of everything necessary for an advanced economy based on heavy industry. The plan was buffeted by long and stormy arguments. Comrades who argued in favour of setting targets at sensible levels were accused of defeatism. The first figures were optimistic: the later figures flew off the top of all graphs of possibility.

An army of workers arrived in the Ural mountains. Living in tents, sharing beds in shifts, they began to build the biggest metallurgical plant in the world at Magnitogorsk. A massive tractor plant arose in Chelyabinsk. A giant hydroelectric scheme

ABOVE *Workers in heavy industry were exhorted to fulfil increasingly unrealistic production targets.*

LEFT *The vast metallurgical complex at Magnitogorsk in the Urals, one of the showpieces of the First Five-Year Plan. Of the original workforce of 50,000, one-third is thought to have been dekulakized peasants on forced labour schemes.*

was built on the Dnieper river. All over the vast empire, huge new complexes were decreed.

Factory directors competed not just to meet the wildly optimistic production targets, but to 'overfulfil' them. Some even hijacked lorries or ambushed freight trains to get their hands on sparse supplies. This was theft, but it was safer than failing to meet the plan, which could bring dismissal, disgrace – or arrest on a charge of sabotage.

The first big sabotage trial happened in the months leading up to the announcement of the First Five-Year Plan. Fifty-three engineers, three of whom were Germans, were put on trial accused of wrecking equipment, organizing accidents and maintaining links with the capitalist former owners of the Shakhty coal mines in the Donbass. The trial opened in the Hall of Columns in Moscow amid a press campaign clamouring for 'Death to the Wreckers!' The twelve-year-old son of one of the accused was among those demanding the death penalty. Five of them were shot.

Stalin said: 'Shakhtyites are now ensconced in every branch of our industry ... wrecking by the bourgeois intelligentsia is one of the most dangerous forms of opposition to developing socialism.'

Thus, in the first years of the Plans, thousands of engineers and 'bourgeois specialists' were arrested and imprisoned, scapegoats to explain away the difficulties of those hard times. Officials were

ABOVE LEFT *Competition between factories was intense. Pressure to top the production league-table led some factory bosses to falsify their figures or steal supplies.*

tried for sabotaging food supplies, which was a good way of explaining the shortage of bread and sausage in the shops. But the true reason for food shortages was government policy. Hand in hand with industrialization came the declaration of class war against the peasantry.

Every industrial revolution requires a massive shift of population from the country to the towns. Factories need workers: workers who have to be recruited and who have to be fed. In the Soviet Union there was one source of both recruitment and food – the peasantry.

The countryside was an apparently bottomless source of hands. Seventeen million people made the journey to the towns during those years. Illiterate, wretched, hungry, pushed around by a new

BELOW *The Shakhty trial in session. Stalin found the idea that engineers were conspiring to sabotage the Five-Year Plans most convenient. Indeed, it explained away the deficiencies of Soviet industry so effectively that other 'wreckers' were put on trial. Among them, in 1933, were six British engineers, employees of the Metro-Vickers company.*

ABOVE *The Dnieper Dam hydroelectric scheme was one of the achievements of the First Five-Year Plan. So great was its value both to the economy and to the morale of the people of the Soviet Union that, in 1941, the dam was deliberately breached to prevent the German invaders from using it. The rebuilt dam was opened in 1947.*

ruling elite which despised them, these peasant hordes became the new working class of Russia.

Nine out of ten of them had only three years of primary-school education. The first director of the Stalingrad tractor factory found his workers using their fingers to measure the precision sockets they were grinding. At the Moscow Elektrozavod works, an American spindle lathe which had cost $25,000 lay idle and rusted, because nobody knew how to mend a simple fault.

Industry began to sound like a battlefield, as thè Party spoke of fronts, campaigns, breakthroughs and shock-workers. The most celebrated of all shock feats was achieved by a Ukrainian miner, Alexei Stakhanov, who hewed 102 tonnes of coal in one shift, instead of the planned seven tonnes. The record was a bit of a

LEFT *The Moscow metro. Nikita Khrushchev, then First Secretary of the Moscow City Party Committee, received the credit for its completion in record time.*

BELOW *Stalin opens the metro in 1935. Its construction, begun four years earlier, provided work for factories all over the USSR. According to a modern tourist guide to the system, 'The entire land pitched in to help build the Moscow metro.'*

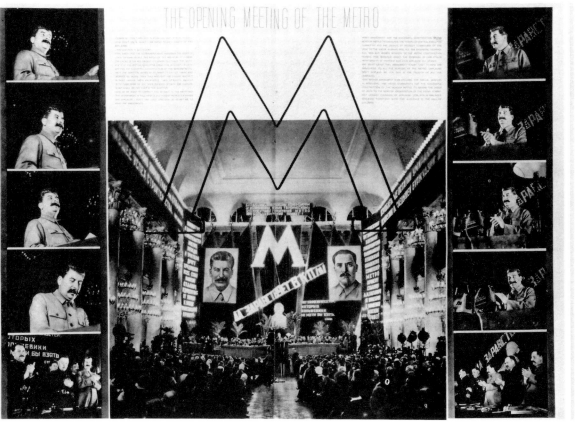

RIGHT *Alexei Stakhanov, the Donbass miner, after the record-breaking stint at the coal-face. His feat of hewing 102 tonnes in a single shift was soon surpassed – one rival notched up 311 tonnes. But it was Stakhanov who gave his name to the language, and 'Stakhanovites' were hailed as the shock-troops of the industrialization drive.*

BELOW *New mothers express their breast milk at the factory. Millions of women were encouraged to combine motherhood with full-time work.*

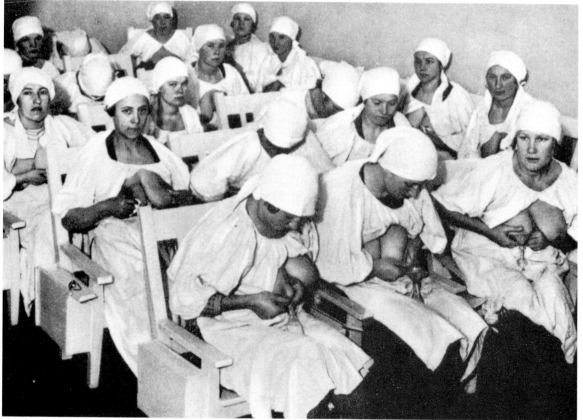

cheat. A gang of his colleagues supported his attempt by taking on all the auxiliary work a faceworker usually has to do. Even so, Stakhanov was decorated by Stalin and lionized by the Soviet media, as the living image of their message: 'There are no fortresses Bolsheviks cannot storm.' The Stakhanovite ideal went down less well with the workers. There were cases of lynchings, especially when the shock-workers began to enjoy privileges like huge pay rises and smart new flats.

Conditions were uncomfortable, miserable and often dangerous. The discipline of an eight-hour day was hard to learn for country people accustomed to the very different rhythms of rural life. Strikes were not allowed, and the trade unions were by now just another arm of the state. So, when workers wanted to show displeasure, they produced rubbish on purpose in a sullen show of disobedience, or simply wandered off in search of a better chance. The average length of time a worker stayed in a job in the coal and iron industries in 1930 was just four months.

To deal with this labour discipline problem, the First Five-Year Plan was accompanied by an escalating succession of restrictive laws. Absenteeism was punished. From 1930, a system of internal passports and permits was introduced, which meant that no town dweller could move to another town without police permission.

However hard their lives, it is likely that most of the new workers did not regret leaving the farms. Industrialization would only be possible if the peasants left behind on the land produced more food to feed the towns. This they seemed unwilling or unable to do. The Party's response was to dust down a policy that had been mouldering on the ideological shelf.

Peasants sign on at a collective farm.

There had been a few small voluntary collectives since the revolution, set up along socialist principles. No socialist ideals were involved in the decision to adopt a policy of compulsory collectivization. It stemmed from a belief that the peasantry harboured a truly capitalist element which meant to strangle Soviet power by starving it. The policy was designed simply to make it easier for the state to get more food out of the peasants.

One result was millions of deaths. Another was a legacy of unproductive farming and resentful farmers which keeps the Soviet Union hungry to this day.

The Communist Party had never trusted the peasants. Though

The collectivization programme moved at breakneck speed. In just three months, 10 million families were forced to join.

Former peasant children learn the rudiments of collective farming.

Villagers in the Caucasus learn about cow husbandry from a travelling expert. Twenty-five thousand young Party activists went to the villages. Among their tasks: to compel peasants to hand over grain.

BELOW *Grain being delivered to a central store. The objective of the requisitioning programme was to secure supplies for people living in towns.*

Lenin had welcomed their revolutionary activity during the heat of 1917, his theory was always that they would revert to their old bourgeois ways as soon as the crisis had passed. As early as 1921, *Pravda* proclaimed: 'A conflict with one million reactionary peasants awaits.'

Before the revolution, the great estates and the richest peasants had produced more than two-thirds of the grain which went to market. Now the great estates and the rich peasants were no more. The bulk of the grain was produced by ordinary peasants, who ate most of what they grew. None of the industrial goods they might have wanted were being manufactured, and the price they got for their grain from the state did not even cover the costs of production. With nothing to buy and prices so low, the peasants were better off growing less grain and eating it themselves, and that is what they did. In 1928 the towns simply went hungry.

The grain crisis took the leadership completely unawares. The Politburo voted unanimously for emergency measures. Thousands of young town dwellers were mobilized and sent into the

Two Stalinist campaigns converge: a grain store in a closed-down church.

country in requisitioning squads. These young Communists recruited help from locals, who took them round the village, poking sticks into cellars and ripping into hidden sacks to find and claim the grain which the Party believed was being hoarded.

Stalin had come up with a new piece of socialist theory to back up the attack on the villages. He argued that the closer a country approached the achievement of socialism, the sharper the class struggle would become. This theoretical intensification of the class struggle was accompanied by his practical guide to help Communists identify a class enemy when they saw one.

Peasants were divided into three grades: poor, middle and kulak. The poor peasants owned nothing and worked on other people's land for wages, which according to Party theory ought to make them allies of the working class and the Party. Middle peasants owned and produced enough for their needs, but no more. 'Kulak', the Russian word for 'fist', was used in pre-revolutionary times to describe a village moneylender. Now the term was intended to cover peasants who had more than they needed and exploited others. The categories were neat, but they were nonsense.

No proper official economic classification of how to identify a kulak was ever agreed. There were a lot of discussion documents arguing whether a kulak was someone who owned two cows or three, whether a person who let a room in her house was a kulak, how many days a year a farmer could hire labour before he became a kulak. There was even a category called 'ideological kulak', which covered anyone who expressed sympathy for their fate. It is hard to escape the conclusion that a kulak was anyone the government chose to name as a class enemy.

Andrean Chernenkov, now eighty-seven and still living in his Don Cossack village of Starocherkassk, was a fisherman from a poor peasant family. He remembers joining in a requisitioning band. 'We went round to the next village taking grain. When I got home that night, my mother was in tears. "Where have you been?" she said. "While you were out they came here and took all our grain, and now we have nothing."'

The peasants did resist. There was looting, civil disorder and riots. Hundreds of Party officials and procurement agents were assassinated. Peasants buried their grain in haystacks or in churches, or sold it illegally to smugglers, or burned it, or threw it into the river. Those who could not or would not meet the demands were dispossessed of their land and deprived of the right to vote.

The next year, 1929, even less grain was collected in spite of the increasingly harsh measures, and requisitioning of meat began. Rationing was introduced in the towns.

The Party made it clear where they put the blame, in the now customary military imagery. They said the rural sector had

Terror in the countryside. The slogan was: 'We demand collectivization and the liquidation of the kulaks as a class.'

At village meetings, like this one in Kazakhstan, suspected kulaks were harangued, humiliated and dispossessed by Party activists. The Stalinist history schoolbook, The History of the Communist Party (Short Course), *justified the persecution: 'The peasants chased the kulaks from the land, dekulakized them, took away their livestock and machinery, and requested the Soviet power to arrest and deport the kulak.'*

The much-celebrated introduction of tractors was offset by a dramatic shortage of the countryside's traditional beast of burden: more than half of Russia's horses died or were systematically slaughtered during the drive for collectivization.

opened a 'second front' against the state, being engaged in a 'livestock offensive' as well as a 'grain offensive'. Wasyl Hryshko, a Ukrainian now living in the USA, remembers the atmosphere of that summer of 1929 in his village. 'We all felt it. There hadn't been any announcement, but we just knew something was going to happen.'

The press began to talk of mass collectivization.

The activists who had spent all the autumn of 1929 failing to procure enough grain were told to stay put and turn their attentions to collectivization. Thousands more Party members set out to join them. These were fervent people who believed they were fighting a war to liberate Soviet power from the stranglehold of an enemy class. The peasants understood very well what their goal was. It was to reorganize everyone out of the land holdings they had won in the revolution, dispossess them and get them into collective farms where their grain would be easier to steal. So it was unthinkable that the peasants would give up their independence voluntarily. Nikolai Bukharin, Stalin's major theoretical opponent, forecast: 'He will have to drown the risings in blood.'

On 27 December, Stalin raised the stakes again. He declared that the aim was the liquidation of all kulaks: 'We must smash the kulaks, eliminate them as a class ... We must strike at the kulaks so hard that they will never rise to their feet again.' He had just turned fifty years old, and birthday greetings in the Party press had hailed him as the greatest Marxist-Leninist who had ever lived.

A secret police report of February 1930 from the Smolensk area gives a matter-of-fact account of how Stalin's directive on 'dekulakization' was put into practice by the workers' brigades and low-level officials of the Party and soviets. Their slogan was 'Drink, eat – it's all ours.' If they found any food they ate it on the spot. Drink went the same way. They took the shoes off children's feet, warm underwear straight off the bodies of their parents. The same secret police report quoted one young Communist who was appalled by the scenes. 'We are no longer people,' she said. 'We are animals.' Another said: 'The best and hardest workers of the land are being taken away, with the misfits and lazybones staying behind.'

One man came home to find all his property removed except for a kettle, a saucer and a spoon. He was arrested and sent to the deadly lumber camps of the far northern forests. Another old man took a photo of his home as he left it. He was arrested and shot the same evening.

The Politburo planned for the dekulakization of five to six million people, and many local Party committees enthusiastically

Propaganda campaigns portrayed life on the collective as idyllic.

overfulfilled their plan. Stalin later remarked to Churchill that dekulakization had been a matter of ten million people.

Whole villages were picked up, put on cattle trains and dumped in the middle of the Arctic north. The secret police were in charge of transporting them. They called their cargo 'white coal'. Many of the victims never made it to their destination: those who did became the backbone of the Stalinist economy. Millions ended up in slave labour camps, building huge civil engineering projects like the canals, lumbering in the far north, or flung into the far eastern wilderness to open up the mineral riches of Stalin's Siberian frontiers. The novelist Ilya Ehrenburg wrote: 'Not one of them was guilty of anything; but they belonged to a class which was guilty of everything.'

Those left behind entered a maelstrom of suffering and resistance. In a typical case, a Ukrainian woman tossed a burning sheaf onto the thatched roof of her house. 'We worked all our lives for our house, you won't have it!' she told the secret policemen. 'The flames will have it.'

This photograph appeared in a book about the Belomor canal by the distinguished writer Maxim Gorky. He was pressed into service to present a cheerful picture of the labourers' conditions to the outside world. Thus, the caption reads: 'Guns are held like this, not to frighten anyone, but simply out of convenience.'

Wild rumours circulated: the women were to become communal property, the children would all be sent away to China, the old people would be burned in a special machine to stop them eating, the Antichrist was coming, the end of the world was nigh. During the spring of 1930 fourteen million cows and a third of all the pigs in the Soviet Union were slaughtered by their owners in a mass refusal to donate a free gift to the collectives.

The Party claimed that half of all households had been collectivized that spring. But the countryside was in chaos. Nothing was being sown.

On 2 March 1930 Stalin wrote an article for *Pravda* in which he accused local officials of proceeding too fast, of being 'dizzy with success'. Half of all the new collectives collapsed, and the peasants got back to work. But as soon as the harvest was safely gathered in, the campaign began anew. There was no escape.

The immediate results of forced collectivization were nothing short of disastrous. Productivity tumbled, while state demands rose sharply. In the Ukraine, local Communists warned Moscow

The dark side of Stalin's modernization campaign: slaves at work on the canal. So harsh were the conditions that 100,000 people may have died. Yet the canal proved too shallow for the ships of the Baltic Fleet, for whose use it had been designed.

that this would result in starvation. But there was a saying at the time: 'Moscow does not believe in tears.'

One young Communist reported from a village near Kharkov that he could make the meat deliveries, but only with human corpses. There were decent officials who gave food to the starving, but this was described in a Party report as 'a waste of bread and fish'.

Those who survived tell stories of unimaginable horror. Mothers killed and ate their children. Human flesh was sold at

Happy days: Stalin with a group of farmers in 1933. Only a few months earlier, the countrypeople of the USSR had struggled to survive the horrors of famine and forced collectivization.

market. The dying dragged themselves to the lips of the pits dug for mass graves and lay there, waiting for the end.

People ate mice, ants, earthworms, bark. They dug up dead horses. They ground bones and leather shoes into a kind of flour. Starving people appeared illegally in the towns and lay about the streets, begging for help. In Kiev, Kharkov, Dniepropetrovsk and Odessa, the local authorities sent carts out at dawn every day to collect the bodies.

In Kazakhstan in Central Asia, collectivization was accompanied by the forced settlement of the nomadic native herdsmen. Forbidden to continue their traditional lifestyle, Kazakhs slaughtered millions of their beasts and tried to escape over the border to China. They fought their way past Russian border guards who included the future Party leader Konstantin Chernenko. Thousands wandered the steppe, dying of starvation.

As the famine raged, the USSR carried on exporting grain. At Reshetilovka station, near Poltava, peasants could see supplies piled up in the open and left to rot, guarded by secret policemen. Several thousand tons of potatoes went bad in a field surrounded by barbed wire. In May 1933, hungry villagers looted a grain warehouse in Sahaydaky. Some died on the way home, too weak to carry their booty, and the rest were shot or imprisoned.

All this time the requisitioning continued, carried out by Party officials convinced that in a class war, the end justifies the means. Some were thugs, some were idealists. Lev Kopelev, now a distinguished dissident writer, believed he was right as he tested the Ukrainian earth with an iron rod to locate buried grain, or turned over the homes of elderly peasants while the women wept and their grandchildren screamed.

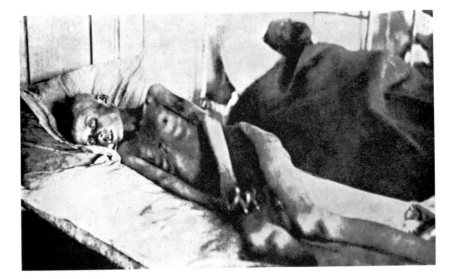

The horror of famine, 1932.

The drive for industrialization was underpinned by a massive literacy campaign. In the first ten years of Soviet rule, half a million people were taught to read and write.

'In the terrible spring of 1933 I saw people dying from hunger. I saw women and children with distended bellies, turning blue, still breathing, but with vacant, lifeless eyes . . . I saw this and did not go out of my mind or commit suicide,' Kopelev remembers. 'Our great goal was the universal triumph of Communism, and for the sake of that goal everything was permissible – to lie, to steal, to destroy hundreds of thousands and even millions of people.'

Five million Ukrainians and a quarter of the entire Kazakh nation perished. The famine which claimed their lives was entirely man-made. It left Soviet agriculture in ruins, and the peasantry finally terrorized into submission. And it left Stalin free to find new targets.

JRSS EN CONSTRUCTION

ABOVE '*Uncle Joe*' *thanks the youth of the empire. Pictures like this were published in a glossy magazine issued to publicize the achievements of the Five-Year Plans.*

RIGHT *Stalin's wife, Nadezhda Alliluyeva, after her death in November 1932. After fleeing from a banquet celebrating the fifteenth anniversary of the October Revolution, she shot herself with a little Walther pistol which her brother, Pavel, had brought her from Berlin. Her daughter, Svetlana, says that her mother left a terrible letter for Stalin, full of reproach and accusation, both political and personal.*

4 Enemies of the People

O n the dark and snowy afternoon of 1 December 1934, an unemployed thirty-year-old Communist called Leonid Nikolayev put a revolver in his pocket and went inside the Smolny Institute in Leningrad. The former school for aristocratic young ladies was still the headquarters of the Communist Party in the northern capital, and there should have been guards on every corner. But Nikolayev wandered unchallenged through the long corridors, and hid in the toilet on the second floor. The man he was waiting for was the city Party Secretary. When he heard his target approach along the corridor towards his office, Nikolayev jumped out of his hiding place and shot his victim in the back of the neck.

The assassination of Sergei Kirov was a decidedly murky affair. Nikolayev had a fat secret police file chronicling his grudge against the Party hierarchy. He had already been arrested twice in possession of a gun in the vicinity of the Smolny. The Institute guards were unaccountably absent. And Kirov's devoted personal bodyguard was killed in a highly suspicious road accident before he could give evidence.

Opinions still differ about whether Stalin ordered the murder of his nearest rival. But there is no doubt that the killing gave Stalin a perfect opportunity to launch his party and his country into a spiralling nightmare of denunciation, mass arrest, execution and terror.

Kirov was a popular leader, energetic, practical and an effective orator. He was as ruthless as any top bureaucrat, but had a reputation for getting things done. His office in the Smolny in Leningrad had no propaganda on the walls. Instead, his massive table looked more like an engineer's desk, covered with models of oil tanks and details of machines. He had been a convinced supporter of Stalin during the collectivization and industrialization period, but now he was beginning to get a name as someone who favoured a breathing space for the tired and hungry population. Nikita Khrushchev, soon to be promoted to First Secretary in Moscow, witnessed fierce arguments between Kirov and Stalin. They quarrelled about the low level of rations in Leningrad, with Kirov arguing that workers worked better with full bellies.

In January 1934, Kirov was the star of the Seventeenth Party Congress. The 'Congress of Victors' took place in a heady atmos-

ABOVE RIGHT *Sergei Mironovich Kirov. Born 1886; organizer of a strike in Siberia 1905; veteran of the October Revolution in Petrograd; defender of Astrakhan in the Civil War; the man who nationalized the Baku oilfields; First Secretary of the Leningrad Party from 1926; assassinated in Leningrad 1 December 1934.*

RIGHT *Kirov lying in state. After the murder, Stalin exacted particular retribution on Leningrad. Of forty signatories to the city's obituary of Kirov in* Pravda, *the top eleven were shot.*

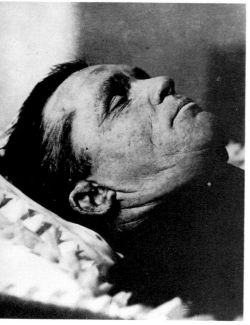

ABOVE *Kirov's ashes on their way to the Kremlin wall in Moscow for burial. At the 22nd Party Congress in 1961, a delegate said of those behind the murder: 'It is as if they had been waiting for this pretext in order, by deceiving the Party, to launch anti-Leninist, anti-Party methods of struggle to maintain a leading position in the Party and state.'*

phere of self-congratulation and unity. Former oppositionists were allowed to speak, and they all repented with abjectly orthodox speeches in praise of Stalin. But backstage, a group of senior delegates was trying to persuade Kirov to stand against Stalin as an alternative General Secretary.

When Kirov refused the invitation, he had less than a year to live. But he was not the only casualty. There were 1966 delegates at the congress. By the time of the next Party Congress five years later, 1108 of the delegates had been shot.

Some of the Old Bolsheviks, those people who had joined the Party before the revolution, had been worried for a long time about the atmosphere since Stalin had taken over. Nikolai Bukharin, the editor of the newspaper *Izvestia*, described a 'real dehumanization of the people working in the Soviet apparatus'.

He thought the Party changed after the unthinkable cruelty of the attacks on the countryside. He noticed 'deep changes in the psychological outlook of those Communists who participated in this campaign, and who, instead of going mad, became professional bureaucrats for whom terror was henceforth a normal method of administration, and obedience to any order from above a high virtue'.

But Bukharin, the most powerful among the moderate critics of Stalin, had recommended no action against him. This was not good enough for some of those who shared Bukharin's views. In late summer 1932, a document began to circulate among the leading lights of the Party. It was two hundred pages long. Fifty pages were devoted to a personal condemnation of Stalin: 'the evil genius of the Russian revolution who, motivated by a personal desire for power and revenge, brought the Revolution to the verge of ruin'. The Ryutin Platform, as the document was called, urged the liberation of the peasantry and the immediate readmission of all expelled members, including Trotsky.

Stalin chose to regard this as a call for his own assassination, and seized the advantage. For the first time he accused oppositionists of capital crimes, and demanded the death penalty for Ryutin, a former Moscow Party boss. The Politburo was still capable of being appalled, and still capable of voting against Stalin. He lost the motion.

Ryutin and his comrades were imprisoned and expelled from the Party as degenerates, traitors and bourgeois kulaks. Zinoviev and Kamenev were once again expelled for a year and deported to the Urals. The following year, 800,000 people were thrown out of the Party. But the Ryutin case did not lie down. It was to reappear time and time again in evidence against Communists at the massive show trials still to come. And the Politburo would not stand up to Stalin for much longer. Once Kirov was killed, opposition became a fatal condition.

Stalin led the offical state mourning for the assassinated leader.

ABOVE *Stalin said to be signing a death warrant in 1933. Later, as the Terror intensified, Stalin is said to have signed lists of people to be executed every day.*

BELOW *The Lubyanka, Moscow. The prison was in an inner courtyard of the secret police headquarters. Moscow purge victims were also taken to the Lefortovo Prison, the main torture centre, or the Butyrka, where 30,000 prisoners could be held, three to the square yard. Prisoners are said to have found a simple way of identifying where they were: they looked at the flooring, which was different in each gaol. If they found themselves walking on a parquet floor, they knew they were in the Lubyanka.*

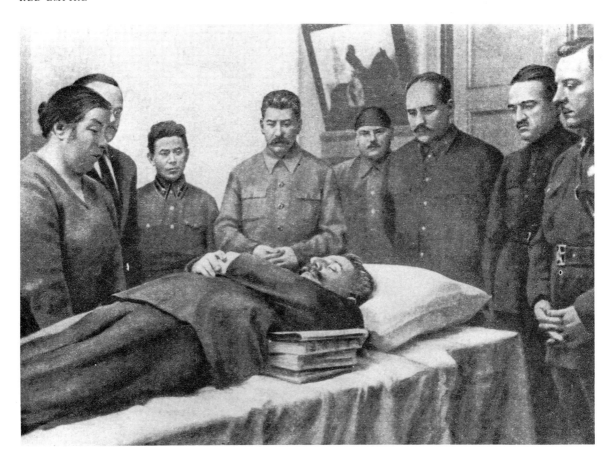

He even interrogated Nikolayev himself. Towns were renamed after the dead hero, and one of the Soviet Union's most prestigious ballet companies also took his name. But the shot that killed Kirov was the trigger of a deafening chorus of retribution. Over the next four years, thousands would be charged as 'murderers of Kirov', and millions more suffer the extreme penalty for alleged conspiracy. The Terror had begun.

It started immediately the dying man was found. All over the country, a great wave of arrests swept into the prisons and death cells anyone who appeared in the secret police files. Thousands of Leningraders were deported to Siberia and the Arctic.

Laws began to change. On 7 April 1935, a decree extended all punishment, including the death penalty, down to twelve-year-old children. This was a carefully calculated move. Stalin could now threaten oppositionists quite legally with the death of their children.

The first of the big show trials began on 19 August 1936, in the October Hall of the Trade Union House, formerly a ballroom of the Nobles' Club. There was room for 150 carefully chosen Soviet citizens and thirty equally carefully chosen foreign cor-

Sergo Ordzhonikidze, a 'hidden' victim of the purges. Was he murdered on the orders of Stalin, seen here with (left to right) Ordzhonikidze's widow Zinaida, Molotov, Yezhov, Zhdanov, Kaganovich, Mikoyan and Voroshilov? The doctors diagnosed a heart attack, but rumours suggested he was poisoned or, as Khrushchev reported, 'forced to shoot himself'.

RIGHT *A Moscow courtroom in the 1930s. The Stalinist show trials were decked out with all the trappings of legality.*

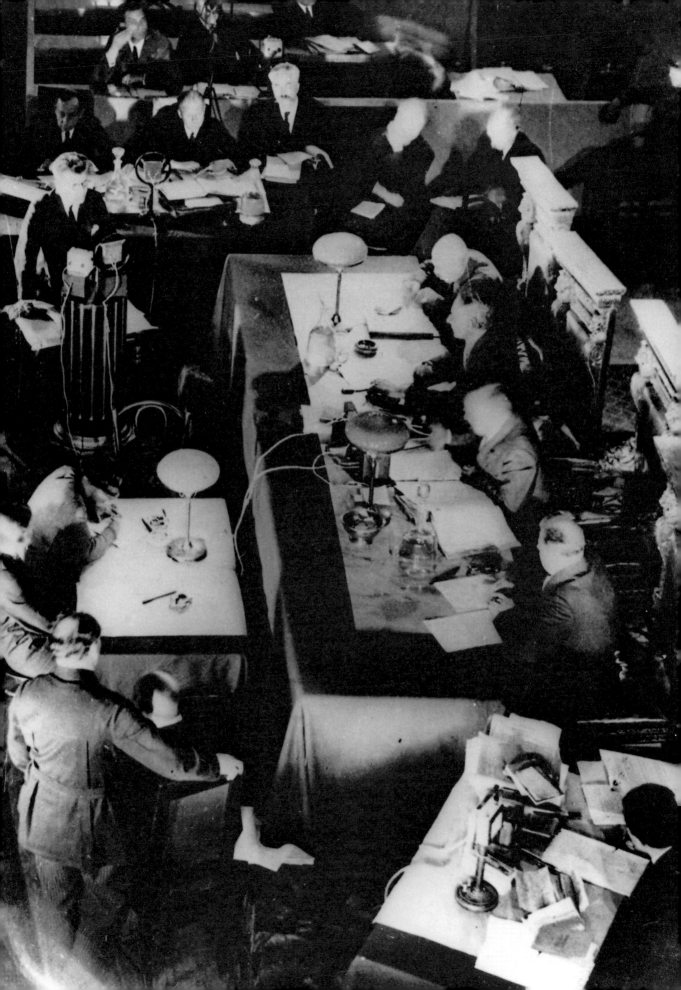

State Prosecutor Andrei Vyshinsky summing up at the Zinoviev/Kamenev trial in 1936. His accusations were preposterous and the language in which he couched them scabrous. He later went on to become Foreign Minister and the USSR's representative at the United Nations.

respondents and diplomats. Relatives of the accused were not allowed in.

The star defendants were Zinoviev and Kamenev, the two Old Bolsheviks who had been in and out of Party favour for years. They stood in the dock charged with terrorist and Trotskyist crimes, including the murder of Kirov. Much of the evidence was laughable. One of their co-defendants confessed to meeting Trotsky's son Sedov at the Hotel Bristol in Copenhagen. From his Mexican exile, Trotsky himself immediately denied this, and the Danish Social Democratic Party later pointed out that the hotel in question had been demolished almost twenty years before.

Prosecutor-General Andrei Vyshinsky demanded the death sentence for these 'mad dogs of capitalism'. The accused made last pleas from the dock. Kamenev said he wanted to send a message to his two sons. 'No matter what my sentence will be, I in advance consider it just. Don't look back. Go forward. Together with the Soviet people, follow Stalin,' he said, and sat down, his head in his hands. All the defendants were sentenced to death, and executed within twenty-four hours of the verdict. One of their judges, Divisional Military Jurist Nikichenko, was to sit in judgement ten years later over Hermann Goering at the post-war Nuremberg tribunal.

Stalin had prepared carefully for his assault on the Party and society. His nominees were in charge in all the key areas of the

Grigory Zinoviev confessed at his trial: 'My defective Bolshevism became transformed into anti-Bolshevism, and through Trotskyism I arrived at Fascism. Trotskyism is a variety of Fascism, and Zinovievism is a variety of Trotskyism.'

BELOW *Trotsky, exiled in Norway, listens to news of the Zinoviev/Kamenev trial on Moscow Radio. The judge ordered his immediate arrest should he return to Soviet territory.*

BELOW *This photograph, issued to the foreign press after the 1936 show trial, shows workers in the turbine shop of the Kirov factory, Leningrad, listening to a report on the fate of Zinoviev and Kamenev. The caption reads, 'Soviet toilers unanimously approve sentence on ringleaders of counter-revolutionary Trotskyist-Zinovievist bloc.'*

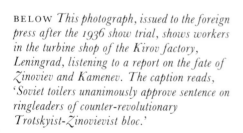

Party apparat and the important cities. In the summer of 1934, he had once again renamed and reorganized the secret police. The new NKVD was run by Genrikh Yagoda, and its emblem was a serpent struck down by a sword.

Since the establishment of the Cheka in December 1917, the secret police had been through several names and changes of leadership, but their influence had steadily grown. The excesses of the Cheka had been one of the main complaints of the ill-fated Kronstadt rebels, who described the organization as many times more horrible than the tsarist gendarmerie. But the Cheka had never been afraid to defend themselves, and Lenin backed them up. He attacked 'a narrow-minded intelligentsia' in the Party who 'sob and fuss'.

He had justified the harsh and bloodthirsty approach of the organization as necessary in a time of civil war. But after the war was ended, the Cheka were even busier, putting down riots and rebellions in all corners of the empire, shooting some participants and sending others to the growing network of concentration and labour camps. Once the disruption of the collectivization years began, the secret police found their hands fuller than ever. In 1934, the NKVD was put in charge of the massive and growing network of labour camps where surviving prisoners were dumped: the Gulag.

Forced labour has a long history in Russia. Tsar Peter the Great used it to build Leningrad. 'Assemble a few thousand thieves for next summer all over the provinces and cities,' he decreed in 1703.

As operated by the NKVD, the Gulag was a crucial part of the new economic order. The prisoners were used to open up vast areas of the country where natural resources were in theory rich, but dangerous and expensive to get at. In the Siberian goldfields of Kolyma and in the Arctic lumber camps of Kotlas, few exposed to the northern cold and damp survived more than a couple of years. All over the empire mining and logging camps were staffed by sick and starving people, their food and clothing issued strictly in accordance with their output. For the Gulag too was subject to the iron discipline of the economic plan, under strict instructions to fulfil its production targets.

This entire economic system was in place well before the Terror of 1937 and 1938. The first prisoners had arrived in Arctic Vorkuta in May 1931, kulaks mostly, travelling almost fifteen hundred miles from Archangelsk by sea and boat up the Pechora river. In the late 1930s, the toiling peasants were to be joined by thousands of victims of the Terror, roused from their beds by the knock at the door, torn from their children, humiliated and tortured, and delivered up to the NKVD and the slave camps.

While the next show trial was being planned, Stalin turned the screw ever more tightly. Resting at his holiday home in the Black

Hard labour on the Ichma River in the northern department of the Gulag. Prisoners, known as 'zeks', mined gold, felled trees and laid railways in some of the remotest regions of Stalin's empire.

The last of the Gulag: the remains of a camp in the Chita region in the far east of the USSR. The average population of the camps during the Stalinist era has been estimated at eight million.

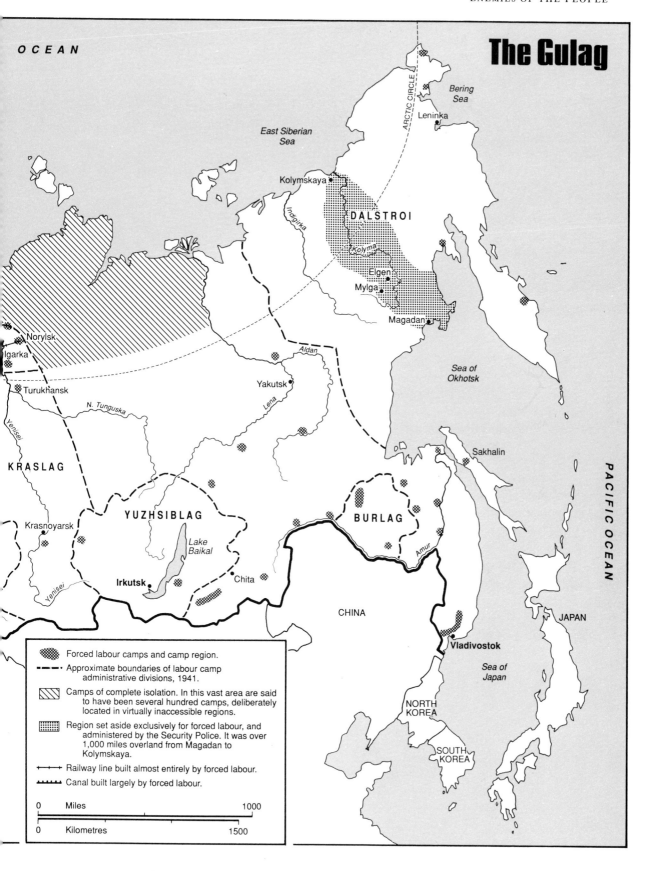

The Gulag

OCEAN

Bering Sea

ARCTIC CIRCLE

Leninka

East Siberian Sea

Kolymskaya

Indigirka

DALSTROI

Kolyma

Elgen

Mylga

Magadan

Sea of Okhotsk

Norylsk

Igarka

Aldan

Yakutsk

Turukhansk

Lena

N. Tunguska

Yenisei

KRASLAG

Sakhalin

Krasnoyarsk

YUZHSIBLAG

Lake Baikal

Yenisei

Irkutsk

Chita

BURLAG

Amur

PACIFIC OCEAN

CHINA

JAPAN

Vladivostok

Sea of Japan

NORTH KOREA

SOUTH KOREA

Forced labour camps and camp region.

Approximate boundaries of labour camp administrative divisions, 1941.

Camps of complete isolation. In this vast area are said to have been several hundred camps, deliberately located in virtually inaccessible regions.

Region set aside exclusively for forced labour, and administered by the Security Police. It was over 1,000 miles overland from Magadan to Kolymskaya.

Railway line built almost entirely by forced labour.

Canal built largely by forced labour.

| 0 | Miles | 1000 |

| 0 | Kilometres | 1500 |

ABOVE LEFT *Stalin and Nikolai Yezhov at the twentieth anniversary of the founding of the secret police in December 1937. Many people blamed Yezhov for the Terror, unable to believe that Stalin was behind it.*

ABOVE *Genrikh Yagoda, Chief of the NKVD secret police, 1934–36. Stalin rewarded him for his zealous application of the Terror by having him tried and shot in 1938.*

Sea resort of Sochi in the autumn of 1936, he sent a telegram to Moscow complaining that the secret police was four years behind in its work. Yagoda was sacked, soon to turn up in the dock on trial for his life, and in his place the fearsome Nikolai Yezhov was appointed People's Commissar for Internal Affairs, head of the NKVD.

The next two years were a whirlwind of death, during which the secret police clawed its way to absolute power as the right hand of Stalin. Yezhov came to seem like a vile hobgoblin, and for many years people blamed him rather than Stalin for the deaths. Many people believed Stalin did not even know about the Terror. The novelist Ilya Ehrenburg tells of meeting Boris Pasternak on a snowy night. Pasternak raised his hands to the dark sky and said: 'If only someone would tell Stalin about it.'

At the end of January 1937, the second big trial began. Former industry minister Grigory Piatakov and another group of Old Bolsheviks stood in the dock at the October Hall, accused of leading bands of wreckers and saboteurs who had blown up mines, railway lines and chemical works. 'This is the abyss of degradation! This is the limit, the last boundary of moral and political decay! This is the diabolical infinitude of crime!' prosecutor Vyshinsky raged.

In his own defence, Piatakov said: 'I stand before you in filth, crushed by my own crimes, bereft of everything through my own fault, a man who has lost his Party, who has no friends, who has lost his family, who has lost his very self.'

When the verdict of death was reached, a crowd of 200,000 assembled in Red Square in a temperature of 27 degrees below zero to hear it announced by Khrushchev, now the Moscow Party Secretary. They carried banners demanding the immediate execution of the sentence.

Early in the new year of 1937, Bukharin's name had appeared for the last time as editor of *Izvestia*. At the end of February, there was a plenum of the Central Committee. Bukharin and former prime minister Alexei Rykov were among those members who made a last attempt to wind up the purge. The moment of their failure is often cited by historians as the point at which Stalin's despotism became an absolute autocracy. As NKVD men waited in the wings, the Central Committee voted in favour of the arrest of the two men, who were dragged off to the Lubyanka, the former headquarters of the Anchor and Lloyd's insurance companies, which the secret police had occupied since 1917. There they were to languish for a year.

Though it took the authorities another year to bring these last top Bolsheviks to trial, the time was not wasted. 1937 was to be the year of ultimate terror, as the NKVD tightened its grip. No section of society was immune. The Terror reached into every village, every home. While the denunciations, the beatings, the torture and the executions went on, Stalin's face gazed down upon his people from every hoarding, and the newspapers were full of reports of the exploits in his honour of brave airmen, explorers and athletic record-breakers.

Seventeen-year-old Ella Shestyer was a bright-eyed Young Communist, full of hopes and dreams for the future of her country's great experiment, when she met and married a fellow student. Raphael Greenberg teased his wife about her love for another man. The pretty young engineering student was devoted to her leader, the father of the nation, whose avuncular half-smile gazed down on her from the posters, promising the shining future for which they all thirsted.

Ella would not hear a word spoken against her beloved Comrade Stalin. When Greenberg told her about Lenin's 'last testament', she refused to believe it and threw a kitchen knife at him. Their arguments became increasingly bitter, until their political differences forced Ella to leave the love of her life. 'We had been told over and over again: Stalin is Lenin today,' she remembers. 'I believed it. But Greenberg was cleverer than me. He said: you wait, he'll shoot the lot of you.'

By the time Greenberg was shot in 1937, Ella had married again. Her second husband loved and trusted Stalin as much as she did. It made no difference. He was shot too. Her children were taken away and she was put on a cattle train east: just one among the countless millions of victims of Stalin's great Terror.

During his two years in power, NKVD chief Yezhov sent Stalin 383 lists containing thousands of names important enough to need his personal signature. Each list was examined by Stalin's prime

minister Molotov. All over the country a lynch-law mentality grew. Individuals were denounced by neighbours and co-workers on an extraordinary scale. Local Party committees held meetings in factories and farms, at which members were encouraged to denounce each other. The dizzying turnover of staff benefited many ambitious young men, including Leonid Brezhnev, who was quickly rising through the ranks of the Dneprodzerzhinsk Party Committee.

In Odessa a single Communist denounced 230 people. In the *Izvestia* office they gave up putting names on office doors: as the messenger girl explained, 'Here today and gone tomorrow.' In such circumstances, it was impossible to trust anyone. A society

ABOVE LEFT *Pavlik Morozov, Stalinist hero. Fourteen-year-old Pavlik, who lived in the village of Gerasimovka in the Urals, became famous in the early 1930s for denouncing his own father, Trofim, to the authorities, for associating with kulaks. This sorry tale was soon publicized and embellished as part of a campaign to encourage young people to inform on their parents. Pavlik's death ensured his fame – which continues to this day. He was stabbed by members of his family while out cranberrying in the woods. Buildings were named after the martyred youth, including the Palace of Young Pioneers in Moscow, biographies speedily written and statues erected.*

ABOVE RIGHT *To Stalin, Mikhail Kalinin had his uses as a figurehead President of the USSR. Kalinin's wife, however, was more dispensable. She was sent to the Gulag. Stalin's exact motives for meting out such brutal treatment to the wife of a close colleague are not clear. One suggestion is that this was a warning of the dangers of stepping out of line.*

of friends and families was shattered into millions of terrified individuals.

They came in the middle of the night. They might be brutal, they might be polite. They searched the flat and bundled the suspect away to the local jail. Prisoners were crowded into filthy, verminous cells. In one case in November 1937, 140 men squeezed into a cell designed for twenty-four. People went down with dysentery, scurvy, scabies and pneumonia.

Then came the interrogation. The central method was called the conveyor. A team of NKVD officers took it in turns to interrogate a suspect round the clock, and they could break almost anyone in a few days. Still, this was expensive in terms of manpower, and as the numbers in jail grew, the conveyor fell out of favour. It was replaced suddenly on the night of 17 August 1937. From now on, people were simply beaten up by fists, boots and table legs.

Everyone had to confess to something, and everyone had to denounce somebody. One Armenian priest with a good memory denounced all the parishioners he had buried in the last three years.

Certain categories of people never stood a chance. Railwaymen were automatically Japanese spies. Engineers were saboteurs. Historians were terrorists. Anyone who had ever been abroad or talked to a foreigner was suspect. National minorities, especially if they lived in Russian towns, were bourgeois nationalists. If in doubt, Trotskyism was a useful catchpenny charge. In this as in all other aspects of Soviet economic life, the quota ruled. Thus, a Tatar woman originally listed as a Trotskyist was reallocated as a bourgeois nationalist, on the grounds that her NKVD captors had exceeded their quota for Trotskyists.

The purges began to take on an increasingly surreal tinge. Astronomers were shot for taking a non-Marxist attitude to sunspots. Census statisticians were shot for publishing figures from which hostile academics could discover the true extent of the population loss after the famine. Nobody was immune. Eventually, even secret policemen were purged.

The charges were 'counter-revolutionary activity', and 'suspicion of espionage'. There was also the chilling accusation of being 'a member of the family of a traitor to the fatherland'. This crime earned many women and children either the death penalty, or exile without right of correspondence. The verdicts were different, but the outcome was the same: all the accused were shot.

Very few people were given anything resembling a trial. In the cellars of the Lubyanka, the condemned simply handed in their clothes and were shot in the back of the neck with a TT eight-shot automatic pistol. A doctor signed the death certificate, the cleaning woman took the bloody tarpaulin away, and the bodies were loaded into vans and taken off for burial in a mass grave.

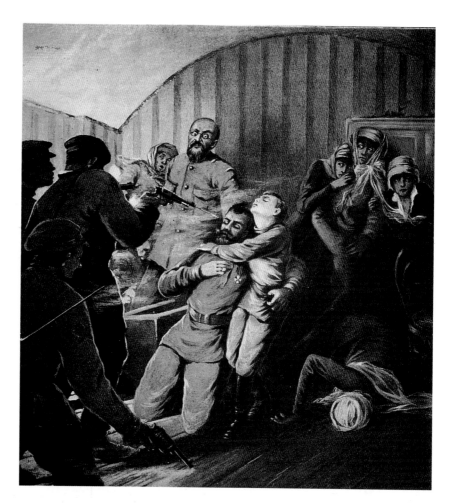

The execution of the Tsar as depicted by White propagandists. The artist, S. Sarmet, based this reconstruction on evidence collected by White Guard investigators two weeks after the disappearance of the Imperial Family in July 1918.

'Lenin Receiving Eastern Leaders' by Nikolai Sysoyev. The Bolsheviks said they favoured a policy of self-determination for the imperial minorities, but Lenin believed the class struggle came before dreams of nationhood. He argued that he sought 'the self-determination, not of peoples, but of the proletariat within each nation'.

An anti-Semitic poster portraying Trotsky as the ogre of the Kremlin. According to a document first published in 1990, Trotsky is said to have anticipated such attacks on the very day of the October Revolution. He apparently told Lenin that his Jewish origins might be a liability to a government trying to establish control in a country where anti-Semitism was rife.

OPPOSITE Propaganda posters. Revolutionary artists helped the Bolsheviks get their message across to a largely illiterate population. White general Baron Petr Wrangel was a frequent target: 'Cossack! You beat Tsar and lord. Now throw Lord Wrangel into the Black Sea!' (top left); 'Devil doll!' – Baron Wrangel is depicted as a puppet of the foreign interventionists (bottom left). Requisitioning squads are encouraged (top right): 'You shed your blood for the worker–peasant revolution! The workers and peasants will deny themselves and give you their last clothes and boots. Take them!' And, at the end of the civil war, workers are urged to greater efforts (bottom right): 'With our weapons we vanquished the enemy. With our labour we will provide bread. Everyone to work, comrades!'

To inspire socialist effort, 1930s' painters found ways to transform everyday industrial labour into art. This socialist realist painting, 'Higher and Higher' by S. V. Ryangina, gives a romantic and heroic picture of electrification.

Socialist unrealism: in the 1920s and 1930s, the discontent, violence and famine of the countryside found no reflection in official art.

A statue of Stalin lords it over the Moscow–Volga Canal. The magazine *USSR in Construction* featured this picture in an issue to mark the opening of the waterway in 1937.

A carpet from the Kirghiz Republic, complete with embroidered portrait, was among thousands of gifts presented to Stalin on his seventieth birthday in 1949. Plans to build an entire museum to exhibit them came to nothing.

The Soviet state, officially atheist from the beginning, encouraged the publication of anti-religious cartoons. The clergy were frequently lampooned for being greedy.

LEFT Red Square, Moscow. The scene of the great set-piece parades of the Soviet state.

RIGHT Stories published after Leonid Brezhnev became Party General Secretary effusively praised his heroic deeds as a political officer during the war. Some said he had embellished his war record as elaborately as his chest.

BELOW Ecological disaster. Misconceived irrigation schemes in the 1960s caused a thirteen-metre fall in the water level of the Aral Sea. This ship, like many others, was engulfed in an ocean of sand.

When he took over as Party leader in 1985, Mikhail Gorbachev inherited the problems and achievements of the world's last empire.

CONSTITUTION
De L'U.R.S.S.

Article 1.—L'Union des républiques soviétiques socialistes est un Etat socialiste des ouvriers et des paysans.

Stalin orchestrated a huge publicity campaign and celebrations when the new Constitution was promulgated in December 1936. Although it was described as a masterpiece rivalled only by Beethoven's Ninth Symphony, the Constitution, which promised improved civil rights and a new electoral system, was never fully implemented.

Stalin greets aviator Valery Chkalov after a record-breaking flight. The celebrations of great feats of Soviet science and exploration offered relief from the tales of treachery coming out of the show trials.

RIGHT *Some heroic ventures went tragically wrong. Three men were killed attempting a high-altitude record in this balloon.*

BELOW *Stalin, seen here at the crew-members' funeral, turned this to advantage. The Stalin personality cult was boosted by the news, from a poet, that the intrepid aviators had died with their leader's name on their lips.*

Those who as children used to play around the old cemeteries of Moscow remember seeing the vans marked 'meat' drive up. They knew the dead were Communists, because all the women had short hair.

The summer of 1937 was unusually warm and sunny, and record numbers of tourists flocked to see the results of the great Soviet experiment. In Leningrad they queued to gasp in disapproval at the tsarist prison cells on display at the Peter Paul fortress, unaware of the terrified people who scurried about the streets, trailing from prison to prison in the vain hope of discovering whether their loved ones were still alive. As the midnight sun lit up the ornate beauty of the old capital, the cellars of the real prisons were full of the damned.

That summer saw the purges reach their zenith when, on 11 June, it was announced that the pride of the Red Army Command had been charged with treason. The next day came the announcement that they had been tried and executed. Among the victims was Marshal Tukhachevsky, the hero of the civil war, who was still only forty-four. *Pravda* reported that the men had all admitted treachery, wrecking and espionage, but no details were ever given. The attrition rate reached 70 per cent of divisional and regimental commanders. The Red Army was decapitated, on the eve of the Second World War.

There is no evidence of any plot against Stalin from inside the army: on the contrary, Khrushchev said later that General Iona Yakir went to his death exclaiming: 'Long live the Party! Long live Stalin!'

Friedrich Engels once wrote in a letter to his old friend Karl

Marshal Tukhachevsky (bottom left) takes the salute at the 1937 May Day parade in Red Square. Eleven days later, he was demoted and executed without any public trial.

A 1930s' photomontage of the Supreme Military Council of the USSR. All except Budyonny (bottom third left) were purged, along with most of the armed forces' top commanders and about half the officer corps – possibly as many as 35,000 men.

Marx: 'Terror consists mostly of useless cruelties perpetrated by frightened people in order to reassure themselves.'

But Lenin had justified the use of terror in certain circumstances, to defend the interests of the proletarian revolution against its enemies. The Bolsheviks regarded their party quite simply as the organized expression of the will of the working class. The interests of the Party were therefore identical with the interests of the revolution. So the defence of the Party, from its enemies within as well as without, was the prime task of the revolution. It was all quite logical. But it was to become the philosophical basis for the unleashing of terror against millions of innocents who found themselves tainted as 'enemies of the people'. Loyal Communists and hardworking idealists fell victim. In the words of a hero of the French revolution, Saint-Just: 'The revolution devours her children.'

The last big trial took place in March 1938. Twenty-one men stood in the dock. They included Bukharin and Rykov, former secret police chief Yagoda, three doctors accused of trying to poison various people, and two Uzbek Party leaders, one of whom had got into trouble for burying his brother according to Muslim rites. The accused confessed to all sorts of things, including causing anaemia to kill 30,000 horses in Belorussia. Several of the defendants put up a spirited defence. But prosecutor Vyshinsky demanded that they be shot like dirty dogs.

'Over the road cleared of the last scum and filth of the past,' he roared, 'we, our people, with our beloved leader and teacher, the great Stalin, at our head will march as before onwards and onwards, towards Communism!'

Lenin's General Statf ot 1917

STALIN, THE EXECUTIONER, ALONE REMAINS

RYKOV	BUKHARIN	SVERDLOV	STALIN	ZINOVIEV	KAMENEV	TROTSKY	LENIN
Shot	Shot	Dead	Survivor	Shot	Shot	In Exile	Dead

KOLLONTAI	URITSKY	KRESTINSKY	SMILGA	NOGIN	DZERZHINSKY	BUBNOV	SOKOLNIKOV
Missing?	Dead	Shot	Shot	Dead	Dead	Disappeared	In Prison

LOMOV	SHOMYAN	BERZIN	MURANOV	ARTEM	STASSOVA	MILIUTIN	JOFFE
?	Dead	?	Disappeared	Dead	Disappeared	Missing	Suicide

The Central Committee of The Bolshevik Party in 1917

462

ABOVE *A gallery of Stalin's victims drawn up by supporters of Trotsky in 1938. Few of Stalin's early colleagues escaped extinction.*

FAR LEFT *Arkady Rosengolts, a former member of Lenin's politburo, stood trial with Bukharin in 1938. In court, Vyshinsky revealed that Rosengolts's wife had sewn a morsel of bread into his hip pocket. Inside was a piece of paper, a tiny good-luck token containing lines from the Psalms:*
'Thou shalt not be afraid for any terror by night: nor for the arrow that flieth by day; For the pestilence that walketh in darkness: nor for the sickness that destroyeth in the noon-day . . .'

LEFT *Nikolai Bukharin, 'star' of the last great show trial, told his wife: 'One day the filter of history will cleanse the dirt from my head.' It took fifty years. Bukharin was finally rehabilitated in February 1988.*

ABOVE *The 17th Party Congress in January 1934. Five years later, Stalin hinted that the Terror had run its course, saying, 'Undoubtedly we shall have no need to resort to the method of the mass purge any more.'*

RIGHT *Victims of Stalin. This mass grave at Chelyabinsk in the Urals was excavated in 1989. More than 80,000 people are thought to have been killed here in the 1930s. The site, known as the Golden Hills, was convenient for the NKVD execution squads because much of the work of digging the mass graves had already been done by goldminers. The bones of the dead have been reburied and a memorial has been set up.*

By the end of 1938, the snowball effect had brought half the entire urban population into the NKVD's files. One in twenty of the population had been arrested. Stalin sacked Yezhov and had him shot. A new man was brought in: Lavrenty Beria, from Stalin's home republic of Georgia. The Terror did not stop altogether, but it did subside.

Robert Conquest's estimate of twenty million victims of Stalinism used to be attacked as inflated by sources both east and west of the old Iron Curtain. Now, Soviet historians accuse him of underestimating the death toll. It is unlikely that a final tally of victims will ever be reached.

Stalin's rivals, especially the cultured people with more than a hint of Russian snobbery in their makeup, always underestimated the man with the withered arm and the strong Georgian accent. The Menshevik Sukhanov, soon to become one of his victims,

RIGHT French philosopher Jean-Paul Sartre, an enthusiastic supporter of Communism, observed that even if reports of Stalin's labour camps were true, their existence should be ignored: 'otherwise the French proletariat might be thrown into despair'.

BELOW George Bernard Shaw, seen here on a visit to the USSR in 1932, was another influential apologist for Stalin. In a letter to The Times, *he opined that the Soviet Union's 'splendid illustrated magazines' provided clear evidence of the benevolence of Stalin's regime. The magazines showed 'crowds of brightly dressed well-fed happy-looking workers ... with their palatial dwellings. Nobody who ever sees these publications,' he asserted, 'will ever believe tales of a half-starved population dwelling in camps under the lash of a ruthless tyrant.'*

described Stalin in 1917 as making no more impression than a grey blur. Trotsky called him 'the most outstanding mediocrity in our Party'.

More careful observers disagree. The Yugoslav dissident Milovan Djilas said Stalin had everything he needed: considerable knowledge of political history and an uncommonly good memory. The dictator's former secretary Boris Bazhanov commented: 'He possessed in a high degree the gift for silence, and in this respect he was unique in a country where everyone talks far too much.'

Nikita Khrushchev was among many Communists who benefited from the purges, winning promotion and favour as the whirlwind roared above his head. He owed his career to Stalin. When he delivered his devastating secret speech of denunciation in 1956, Khrushchev said: 'We cannot say that these were the deeds of a giddy despot. He considered that this should be done in the interests of the Party, of the working masses, in the name of defence of the revolution's gains. In this lies the whole tragedy.'

Stalin liked to finish what he started. On 21 August 1940, his hired hitman Ramon Mercader walked into Trotsky's house in Mexico and dealt him a deadly blow with an ice axe. Mercader got twenty years in a Mexican prison. His mother got a trip to Moscow where Beria presented her with medals for herself and her son.

Trotsky in Mexico, 1938. The artists Diego Rivera (left), Frida Kahlo (second left) and Andre Breton (fifth left) were among his friends.

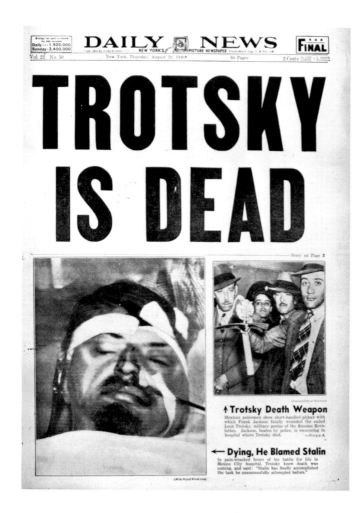

The news of Trotsky's assassination reported in the American press. His assassin described the attack: 'I had put down my raincoat on a piece of furniture. I grasped the ice axe (which I had hidden in the coat) and, closing my eyes, I brought it down on Trotsky's head with all my strength. I thought that after this mighty blow he would be dead at once, but he uttered a terrible piercing cry – I shall hear that cry all my life.'

BELOW *Trotsky's cremation. A few months before his death he had written: 'I shall die a proletarian revolutionist, a Marxist, a dialectical materialist, and, consequently, an irreconcilable atheist. My faith in the communist future of mankind is not less ardent, indeed it is firmer today, that it was in the days of my youth.'*

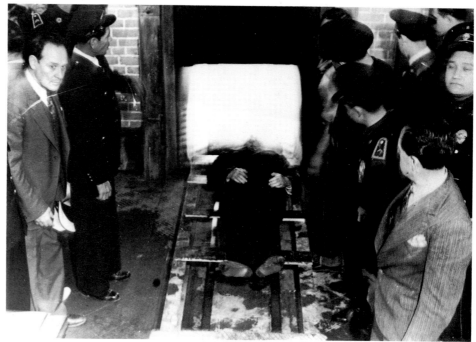

5 Patriots

In August 1939, a Moscow film studio was hurriedly raided by an official who took away the collection of German flags which were being used as props in anti-Nazi films. The flags were needed urgently to welcome Adolf Hitler's Foreign Minister, who was about to arrive in Moscow. Stalin's first words to von Ribbentropp were conciliatory. Both sides had 'poured buckets of filth' over each other for years, he said, but that was no reason not to make their quarrels up now.

The result was the Nazi–Soviet Pact. The Germans got valuable grain and oil imports, while the Russians got promises of military technology. Both sides promised not to attack each other. Communist parties all over the world got a fundamental shock as they suddenly found themselves in close alliance with fascists. And in Eastern Europe, several small nations found themselves part of the Soviet empire.

A picture that shocked the world. Stalin presides over the signing of the Nazi–Soviet non-aggression pact by Vyacheslav Molotov on 23 August 1939.

Under the terms of the pact, the Soviets benefited from German technology and supplied the Germans with oil, copper, rubber and other materials vital to their war effort. Trains like these oil-tankers were still running on the night of the German invasion in 1941.

BELOW LEFT *September 1939: German and Red Army officers discuss their partition of Poland. Molotov said: 'There was one swift blow to Poland, first by the German Army and then by the Red Army, and nothing was left of this ugly offspring of the Versailles Treaty which had existed by oppressing non-Polish nationalities.'*

RIGHT *The Red Army enters eastern Poland. Within a year, Stalin was to annex the Baltic states of Lithuania, Latvia and Estonia, exercising an option granted by secret protocols to the Nazi–Soviet pact. When the documents came to light half a century later, they included a map detailing the 'carve-up' of territory signed by Stalin himself.*

Poland was the first to fall, carved up between the two dictators and subjugated. Red Army and NKVD units moved in, imprisoned thousands of dissenters and set up a puppet government in the beautiful old city of Lvov.

On 14 June 1940, France fell. Next day, the Red Army began to move on the independent Baltic republics of Latvia, Lithuania and Estonia. Again, the NKVD went in to rid the three nations of undesirables. Thousands were tortured, executed or shipped off to the Gulag. At the end of the month, the Romanian province of Bessarabia, later Moldavia, met the same fate. By the autumn, the NKVD had drawn up long lists of twenty-nine categories of persons to be 'registered for later arrest or deportation to Russia'. These included Trotskyists, Jews, stamp collectors and people who spoke Esperanto.

Stalin's next target, Finland, proved more difficult to subdue. In heroic battles among their dark and snowy forests, small units of Finns on skis accounted for thousands of Soviet casualties before they succumbed. But by the summer of 1941, Stalin had control of all the areas promised to him in the secret protocols of the Pact. His agreement with Hitler seemed to be working perfectly.

Finnish ski-troops in the 'Winter War', November 1939–March 1940. The invasion of Finland exposed a Red Army hampered by outdated equipment, its leadership devastated by the purges of experienced officers.

It was only a matter of time. Hitler had always declared that Bolshevism was an odious thing inspired by Jews. He had always said he looked east for Lebensraum, the space for Germans to expand into.

On 22 June a German radio operator intercepted an appeal from a Soviet unit on the western borders: 'We are being fired on. What shall we do?' The reply from Moscow was: 'You must be insane. And why is your signal not in code?'

Almost two years after the signing of the Nazi–Soviet Pact, total war had reached Russia. Three million men attacked without warning before dawn on Sunday, 22 June. Hitler described his Operation Barbarossa as the largest military assault in history.

The Germans were vastly outnumbered by Soviet forces. But they had the priceless advantages of excellent organization and of surprise. The Soviet masterspy Richard Sorge, a German newspaper correspondent working in Tokyo, had warned Stalin in April of the German plan. But Stalin simply did not expect the Führer to turn east when he had not yet defeated Britain.

In the capital, people were waking up to the promise of a perfect summer's day. Radio Moscow was broadcasting the usual Sunday morning fare of children's programmes and popular music. The streets of the city filled with shoppers and sightseers. By the time the news broke at noon, the German army was racing eastwards along a front more than a thousand miles long. Twelve hundred Soviet aircraft were burning, almost all destroyed on the ground by enemy bombing. The destruction was so easy that the Luftwaffe called it infanticide.

It was not Stalin who spoke to the nation on that day. Ivan Maisky, the Soviet ambassador in London, said Stalin locked himself in his office and refused to see anyone. So it was Foreign Commissar Vyacheslav Molotov's voice which crackled out through the loudspeakers on every street corner: 'The Government calls upon you, men and women of the Soviet Union, to rally round the glorious Bolshevik Party and its great leader, Comrade Stalin.'

As the Wehrmacht advanced into the newly annexed countries on the Soviet Union's western borders, the NKVD pulled out. Their orders were to send their prisoners to work in the labour camps, so for days the roads and railways east were packed with thousands of Poles, Ukrainians and Balts.

Where time or inclination did not permit evacuation, the prisoners were killed. In Lvov, several thousand prisoners had been held in three jails. When the Germans arrived on 29 June, the city stank, and the prisons were surrounded by terrified relatives. Unimaginable atrocities had occurred inside. The prisons looked like abattoirs. It had taken the NKVD a week to complete their gruesome task before they fled.

The war was twelve days old before Stalin came back to public

The day war reached Russia: 22 June 1941. Molotov told crowds gathered in the streets of Moscow that the surprise German invasion was 'an unparalleled act of perfidy in the history of civilized nations'.

Villagers who welcomed German troops to the Ukraine soon learned the error of their ways. Hitler regarded all Slavs as subhumans, to be treated as slaves. His SS chief Heinrich Himmler said: 'If ten thousand Russian females die of exhaustion digging an anti-tank ditch, that interests me only insofar as the ditch is dug for Germany.'

Massacre in Lvov, June 1941. Relations of prisoners murdered by the fleeing NKVD, the Soviet secret police, learn the fate of their loved ones.

BELOW *Citizens of Lvov at one of the town's three jails. Radio announcements summoned them to identify the bodies of the prisoners.*

life. His speech at 6 am, Moscow time, on 3 July, was his first address to the nation in three years. He made little mention of rallying round the Party. Addressing his listeners as dear friends, brothers and sisters, he appealed directly and effectively to Russian patriotism.

The conflict the West knows as the Second World War is called the Great Patriotic War in the USSR. There is no doubt that Stalin was right to count on a resurgence of Russian nationalism as the German army swept into the heartland at a rate of fifty miles a day. But, then as now, the Soviet Union had many nations, and many kinds of patriot. Some felt little reason to rally round the red flag.

German soldiers who marched into the Ukraine that summer report that they were welcomed in the traditional way with offers of bread and salt. After the collectivization and famine which nationalistic Ukrainians believed amounted to genocide, many villages felt no loyalty to the Soviet government. They hoped for liberation at the hands of the Germans. They had not read *Mein Kampf*.

Hitler did not regard only Jews as subhuman. He thought the Asiatic influence on Russia had diluted its racial heritage so much that the Slavs, too, counted as 'Untermensch'. German newspapers began publishing photos of Red Army captives, pointing out the 'degenerate-looking orientals'. Hitler's dream was to find homes for one hundred million Germans, and the Ukraine was his major target for the expansion of the Reich. Only the Cossacks were exempt: Hitler had persuaded himself that this

German expectations that public executions would cow the partisans and deter civilian support for them were not fulfilled. Instead, many of the executed partisans became national heroes and heroines. Perhaps the most famous was an eighteen-year-old Moscow girl, Zoya Kosmodemyanskaya. In December 1941, she was tortured and publicly hanged for blowing up a German ammunition dump.

usefully warlike people was not Slav at all. Other natives were beneath contempt.

The German army invasion was followed by the barbarous troops of Heinrich Himmler's Einsatzgruppen. These special task forces came in behind the regular army to exterminate Jews, Communists and other undesirables. One of the four commanders, Otto Ohlendorf, claimed that during the first year his unit liquidated 90,000 men, women and children.

Ukrainians were accustomed to losing families to the Soviet labour camps. Now millions were shipped west to work in the labour camps of the German Reich. Soon Hitler's Minister of Propaganda, Josef Goebbels, was to note in his diary: 'The partisans are in command of large areas of occupied Russia and are conducting a regime of terror there. We have hit the Russians, and especially the Ukrainians, too hard ... a clout on the head is not always a convincing argument.'

In military terms, Barbarossa began as a relentless success. By October the Germans had overrun the Ukraine and stood within sight of Moscow and of Leningrad. Stalin purged and shot even more of his depleted officer corps up to the rank of general, and issued a secret order requiring soldiers to kill themselves rather than surrender. Panic descended in Moscow. The NKVD burned files in the Lubyanka, and the streets were clogged with cars as people tried to escape to the east.

It was not the Russian winter which first stopped the enemy advance, but the rain. In October it began to pour. As troops and vehicles stuck in the mud, officers and men alike prayed for a frost to harden the ground. Their prayers were answered in November, when the snow began to fall.

Stalin took a last-minute decision to go ahead with the traditional 7 November anniversary of the revolution parade through Red Square. Men marched through the square and straight to the front, as Stalin spoke to his troops from the roof of Lenin's mausoleum. He referred to their great ancestors from pre-revolutionary military history, explicitly linking the Red Army with the victories over the Teutonic knights of 1242, the Mongols in 1380, and Napoleon in 1812 – the man each Russian soldier knew was defeated by 'General Winter'.

Every Russian winter is an ordeal, but the winter of 1941 was a record-breaker. The frost came in hard and fast. It froze the German machines. It also froze the soldiers. Before dawn on 7 December, the temperature fell to 28 degrees below zero. Men began to die, their light boots and overcoats no match for the winds sweeping across from Siberia. The 12th Panzer Division reported sixty-three men killed by enemy action and 325 by frostbite. Thousands of frozen corpses lined the Wehrmacht's tracks through the limitless Russian plains.

By the time the Germans reached the Moscow–Volga Canal on

7 *November 1941. The anniversary of the Revolution was marked by the traditional parade. Many of these soldiers had orders to march straight on to the front.*

BELOW *Soviet prisoners of war in the autumn of 1941. Troop losses were so heavy in the early months of hostilities that senior officers were declared incompetent or traitorous, and shot. Stalin's refusal to sign the Geneva Convention meant that Soviet prisoners of war suffered great hardships. Escape or release often made things worse. Many former prisoners of war were executed or re-interned by the NKVD, obeying Stalin's dictum that there were 'no Russian prisoners of war, only traitors'.*

28 November, they had lost three-quarters of a million men, but they were only fifteen miles from the Kremlin. Further south, their troops had captured a quarter of the territory of European Russia, and with it thirteen million workers, three hundred munitions plants and half the cows and horses in the empire.

While the Red Army tried to hold the line, the Communist Party had been throwing its considerable organizational talents into a daring plan to safeguard what was left of Soviet industry. Virtually the whole economy was dismantled and packed off to the east. Herds of cows could be seen being driven through the streets of Moscow, walking hundreds of miles east to safety. Factory workers laboured night and day to unbolt their precious machinery, pack it up in numbered boxes, and load it into trains camouflaged with birch twigs. Tractor factories left Moscow, Kharkov and Leningrad to start a new life manufacturing tanks on the other side of the Urals. By November ten million people had been evacuated with their factories to Siberia and Central Asia.

The Soviet Union had already lost four million prisoners when in early December the Red Army counter-attacked. This time Stalin listened to his brilliant spy, Richard Sorge, who told him the Japanese had no intention of attacking Russia from the east. Two days later the Japanese bombed Pearl Harbor, and the Americans joined the war.

The home front: Moscow, October 1941. Old people, women and children shouldered the burden of defence. Here a huge ditch, one of several encircling the city, is under construction.

ABOVE LEFT *A barrage balloon on Sverdlov Square. Other measures to fool the German bombers included the elaborate camouflaging of public buildings, often under the direction of theatre designers, who used branches and painted canvas to conceal the building's identity.*

LEFT *One of the newly-constructed Metro stations doubling as an air-raid shelter.*

ABOVE *Outside Moscow, December 1941. The cavalry of the Third Guards Division goes into the attack, driving back German soldiers who had claimed to have got near enough to the city to see 'the domes of the Kremlin through a pair of good field-glasses'.*

RIGHT *Victory for 'General Winter' in the battle for Moscow.*

Leningrad under bombardment. During the blockade, which lasted from September 1941 until January 1944, the city's inhabitants endured almost unimaginable privations.

This meant the formidably hardy Siberian divisions could move west. To them, the Moscow winter seemed mild. They were backed by the fast-moving T-34 tank, and by squadrons of cavalry on small Russian steppe horses, who went into battle with sabres drawn. The German General Hinrichs was very impressed when he was attacked in the early morning at 35 degrees below zero. 'The Soviet soldiers remained almost motionless about eight hours lying in the snow. And in the evening they again attacked with the same spirit,' he wrote.

Russians are accustomed to the winter, but they are not super-human. Hitler regarded the old imperial capital of Leningrad as the guilty birthplace of Bolshevism, and therefore deserving of destruction. The blockade he threw around the city in September was to last for nearly nine hundred days. By the end 630,000 Leningraders were dead from cold and hunger, and another 200,000 from German shells.

The siege of Leningrad is a story of unrivalled heroism and endurance. Three million people were trapped inside the city. Under the strict control of Party chief Andrei Zhdanov, they were mobilized to defend it. They worked at their jobs all day and built trenches at night, under a bombardment which lasted nine

In a city without electricity or fuel for transport, bodies had to be dragged to the cemeteries on sledges. Sometimes the effort demanded too much of people's dwindling reserves of strength. Corpses left by the roadside became an everyday sight.

Across the frozen Lake Ladoga, near Leningrad, lorries bring supplies to the starving people within the city. In the spring this lifeline was cut, leaving the city once again to its agony of isolation.

hours of every day. By the autumn there was no food. Electricity was cut off and rations fell to starvation levels. People ate anything. They went through medicine chests in search of vaseline, they scraped paper off the walls to get at the glue. A dog or cat was worth a month's wages on the black market.

As winter approached, their plight was desperate. They built an eighteen-mile road of ice across the frozen Lake Ladoga. The Germans strafed the road continually, but some lorries made it across the lake and food began to come in. Even so, January and February of 1942 saw 200,000 deaths. People simply fell down dead in the street. Theatre producer Grigory Polyachik remembers how the living ignored the dead. 'It sounds inhuman, but you just got used to it. We still put plays on at the Pushkin Theatre, and one day an actor just fell dead on the stage. We shuffled in front of him to hide him, and someone just pulled him into the wings. You had to keep going.'

As Leningrad's agony continued, the army retreated further and further, slashing and burning as it went, leaving nothing but scorched earth and desolation for the advancing Germans.

A thanksgiving service celebrated by the Orthodox Metropolitan Nikolai after the battle of Moscow. During the war, Stalin allowed churches to re-open for services, believing that priests would inspire patriotism.

BELOW *One of the factories evacuated to safety east of the Urals. The workers were expected to begin work immediately, although the construction of their new factory had hardly begun.*

Hitler's prime objective in the summer of 1942 was the capture of the oilfields of the Caucasus. But he was distracted by the continuing existence of a city which bore the name of his enemy: Stalingrad. He became obsessed with the idea of destroying it. Several German generals told him this was a bad idea, so he sacked them. His decision to divert precious forces to take the scruffy industrial town on the Volga was one of the great tactical mistakes of the war.

The former city of Tsaritsyn had been renamed to honour Stalin shortly after Lenin's death in 1924. It was a long thin industrial settlement of half a million people, which stretched for twenty-five miles along the west bank of the Volga. The German General Friedrich von Paulus, commanding 400,000 men, launched a ferocious attack which was to last three months.

The Russians fought street by street, brick by brick. With the waters of the Volga at their backs, they defended every ruined factory and every pile of rubble. Panzer officer Lieutenant Weiner wrote: 'We have fought fifteen days for a single house.' The fighting was so heavy that every leaf fell from the trees. Twenty-two German divisions massed against them, but though the Nazis destroyed the city, they could not vanquish its defenders.

The Red commander at Stalingrad was General Vasily Chuikov, a soldier's soldier, loved by his men, fearless and indestructible. His imaginative guerrilla style of battle unnerved

OPPOSITE *The battle of Stalingrad. The army newspaper* Red Star *reported: 'Often it happens that while the enemy holds one part of a building, we hold another.... The hand-grenade, the bottle of incendiary fluid, the bayonet – such are the weapons which are often used in street and house-to-house fighting.'*

RIGHT *Stalingrad after the battle. A British war correspondent wrote: 'One has become hardened to ruins; one has become bored with ruins. Ruins are monotonous. But in 1943 Stalingrad left one with an unforgettable impression. ... Every inch of Stalingrad was a battlefield. For five months it had been, to use the gruesome but picturesque Russian phrase, a mincing machine, a meat-chopper. Walking over the frozen, tortured earth of Stalingrad, you felt that you were treading on human flesh and bones. And sometimes it was literally true.'*

LEFT *Even the lemonade factories were converted to help the war effort. This production line is turning out the primitive petrol bombs known in the West as 'Molotov cocktails'.*

the Germans. 'Every German soldier must be made to feel that he was living under the muzzle of a gun,' Chuikov wrote. 'The Germans could not stand close fighting ... they fired simply to keep up their morale.'

The probable effect on Soviet morale of losing a city named after the country's leader was not lost on Moscow. As Chuikov and his men fought on, Stalin sent Marshal Georgy Zhukov to the Volga. Their daring plan was not just to relieve Stalingrad, but to deal the German army a blow which would puncture the myth of its invincibility. That autumn Zhukov assembled a mighty force of twelve armies and waited for the ground to freeze. As soon as his tanks could move, he advanced. On the fourth day von Paulus and a quarter of a million men were surrounded.

Hitler forbade von Paulus to surrender. The Germans suffered their encirclement for ten weeks before they gave themselves up. It was 2 February 1943. Two hundred thousand German soldiers were dead, ninety thousand captured, and Russia celebrated one of the greatest victories in its history.

If the battle for Stalingrad was a psychological turning point, in military terms the crucial engagement began six months later. 'The victory at Kursk,' Hitler said, 'must shine like a beacon to the world.' But the great tank battle at Kursk in the summer of 1943 was won by Marshal Zhukov, 1,300,000 men and 3444 tanks. Red Air Force and Luftwaffe planes circled uselessly overhead: the tanks were locked together so closely that the planes could not fire without endangering their own side. The Germans were outnumbered and outclassed. The Soviet victory was a

In the mighty tank battle of Kursk in July 1943, the Germans were out-manoeuvred and out-gunned by a Red Army increasingly confident of ultimate victory.

tribute not just to the valiant tank and infantry divisions, but to the millions of workers who had travelled to the east with their factories in boxes.

The defeats at Stalingrad and Kursk revived a long-standing argument among the Nazi top brass. Not all senior Germans agreed with Hitler that the Slavs were subhuman, and many believed his policy in the east to be shortsightedly cruel and economically impractical. They urged him to make better use of the willing Soviet captives who fought on the German side.

From early in the conflict, Soviet prisoners of war had served the German army as Hilfswillige, or volunteers. Special legions were formed from nationalities including Turkestani, Armenian, North Caucasian, Georgian, Azerbaijani and Volga Tatar, as well as Russian. There was even a Ukrainian unit of the Waffen-SS, known as the Galicia Division. Its ten thousand men swore an oath: 'that in the struggle against Bolshevism I will give the Commander-in-Chief of the German armed forces, Adolf Hitler, absolute obedience, and if it be his will, as a fearless soldier I will always be prepared to lay down my life for this oath.'

Eventually a million Soviet men were fighting under German colours. Three million more worked in the labour camps. What the German dissidents needed was a figurehead. In 1942, they captured one.

General Andrei Vlasov was a member of the Communist Party and a career soldier who had fought on the Red side in the Civil War. He had been awarded the Order of the Red Banner in recognition of his contribution to the defence of Moscow in the

General Andrei Vlasov inspects soldiers of his Russian Liberation Army. A German government official reported: 'His stated objective is to fight as Germany's ally for a socialist Russia and to rid his country of Stalin's system of terror.'

ABOVE LEFT *Food for partisans in a secret hideout. Stalin had called for the creation of these small bands of fighters in his first speech of the war. 'Insufferable conditions must be created for the enemy,' he said. More than a million people responded, fighting alongside the Red Army or wreaking havoc in territory occupied by the Germans.*

winter of 1941. But in the summer of 1942, he was captured by the Germans after a demoralizing and disastrous campaign to relieve Leningrad. The idea of a Russian Liberation Army was born.

The Army had its own insignia, based on the diagonal cross of Russia's patron saint, St Andrew, in pre-revolutionary red, white and blue. It published a call to arms, the Smolensk Declaration, which was dropped into the occupied territories. Its aims were declared to be the overthrow of Stalin, the destruction of Bolshevism, the conclusion of an honourable peace with Germany, and the creation of a new Russia without Bolsheviks or capitalists.

The town of Smolensk was inundated with enquiries from interested deserters. But there was no real Army. Vlasov, a brave but naive man, was a pawn lost on the confusing board of German policy differences.

Hitler lost patience with the idea. He said: 'We will never build up a Russian Army, that is a phantom of the first order.' He did not return to the possibility until it was far too late to be of any use. Vlasov was given two ill-equipped divisions at the very beginning of 1945, but was soon captured by the Americans and handed over to the Russians, who shot him.

Stalin had no mercy for those he termed collaborators. As he reconquered the occupied territories, he took revenge.

The sunny Crimean peninsula had been a favourite holiday destination since tsarist times. Hitler, always on the lookout for suitable places for Germans to live, thought it would make a perfect home for Austrians from the Tyrol.

As in the Ukraine, many Crimean cities welcomed the German forces and hailed them as 'liberators'. Again, the reasons for this

LEFT *Child of the occupation. The young Mikhail Gorbachev, seen here with his maternal grandparents, saw his home village of Privolnoye in the northern Caucasus fall to the Germans in the summer of 1942.*

are not hard to find. As in many imperial trading posts, the people here had always been very mixed ethnically: half were Russians and Ukrainians, a quarter were Crimean Tatars, and the rest were made up of Jews, Germans, Armenians and Bulgarians. But it was the Muslim Crimean Tatars, who settled in the Black Sea peninsula in the Middle Ages, who claimed to have been there longest.

Soviet power had not been kind to them since it was imposed on the territory after the Whites' last stand in 1920. Thousands died as a result of Cheka reprisals and the terrible famine of 1921. There was a few years' grace during the 1920s under the leadership of a Crimean Tatar Bolshevik, Veli Ibrahimov. But when he was shot as a bourgeois nationalist in 1928, thousands were sent off to labour camps, and the cultural identity of the people was stamped out. In the years between 1917 and 1933, the population of the Crimea fell by half, as 150,000 people either died or were forcibly exiled.

As in Lvov, once the Germans advanced on the Crimea, the NKVD shot all its remaining prisoners, and the Red Army retreated, destroying everything it left behind. It was not hard for the Germans to recruit 20,000 Tatars into self-defence battalions and send them into the mountains to hunt Red partisans.

Not all Tatars collaborated with the Nazis. One heroic unit of 250 Red Tatars fought all through 1942 until every one was dead. Thousands more fought as front-line soldiers in the Red Army, and eight were decorated as Heroes of the Soviet Union. None of this helped their compatriots when the Russians reappeared in the spring of 1944.

If any two people accused a Tatar of collaboration, the unfortunate person was executed without trial. The streets of Simferopol were lined with corpses hanging from trees and telephone poles. Entire villages were wiped out. After two weeks of this, retribution was exacted on all the remaining population. On 18 May, every single Crimean Tatar was forced on to a cattle wagon and sent east. Old men, women, children, and four Heroes of the Soviet Union spent up to four weeks on trains, travelling across the scorching heat of the steppe to permanent exile in Central Asia. Thousands died on the journey.

The operation was organized by Ivan Serov of the NKVD, an experienced removal man. He had already directed the mass deportations from the Baltic States in 1939, and the evacuation of industrial equipment from Stalingrad in 1942. He was awarded the title Hero of the Soviet Union and granted the Order of Lenin.

The same terrible fate befell other small southern nations. The Kalmyks, the Karachai-Balkar, the Chechen-Ingush, were all rounded up and deported in secret night-time operations. The Volga Germans, who had lived in Russia since the time of the

BELOW *Lieutenant-General Nikita Khrushchev and Colonel Leonid Brezhnev on the Caucasian front in 1942. The two future leaders of the USSR began to forge close links during the Second World War.*

The return home to rebuild a land fit for heroes and heroines.

BELOW *9 May 1945. The Red Flag flies from the Reichstag in Berlin. The man who took this photograph commandeered an aeroplane to fly to Moscow, thereby ensuring his historic picture made the front page of the next day's* Pravda. *As soon as the paper was off the presses, he flew back to Berlin to show off his scoop.*

The price of victory. Many homeless people lived in holes in the ground for years after the war.

BELOW *The ruins of Murmansk. An American diplomat was appalled by the 'universal, grinding, hopeless poverty of the Russian people' in the aftermath of the war.*

The Yalta Conference. Churchill (left), Roosevelt (centre) and Stalin (right) meet to draw the map of post-war Europe.

BELOW *The victorious leader. One of Stalin's first peacetime acts was to assume the hitherto unknown military rank of 'Generalissimus'. During the war, he had allowed Red Army soldiers to wear decorations and elaborate uniforms reminiscent of tsarist times. An order for vast quantities of braid was accordingly placed with British manufacturers in 1942. It was promptly fulfilled, despite the scepticism of embassy officials who thought the provision of such adornment was frivolous in days of bitter conflict.*

eighteenth-century tsarina Catherine the Great, were sent away to Siberia and Kazakhstan. In all, more than a million and a half people were punished for their national guilt.

Ten great offensives during that year of 1944 liberated huge stretches of Russia and brought the USSR to the brink of victory. The Red Army was a hard school. The soldiers fought with NKVD battalions at their backs, who had orders to shoot malingerers. Marshal Zhukov told General Eisenhower that he used penal battalions to clear minefields with their feet. And theirs was the only army in modern times not to grant home leave. So, as they marched west, the victors could see for the first time the destruction wrought by war and occupation.

In areas of partisan activity terrible cruelties had been committed on both sides. In Belorussia alone, one in four of the population had perished, and 250 villages had been razed to the ground, their occupants herded into the church and set alight. Twenty-five million people were homeless. Countless widows and orphans were living in holes in the ground.

Victory was proclaimed on 9 May 1945, after Soviet soldiers flew the red flag from the Reichstag building in Berlin.

In jail in Moscow, Artillery Captain Alexander Solzhenitsyn realized the war must have ended when the prisoners were given their dinner at the same time as their lunch: something which usually only happened at the Lubyanka on the holidays of May Day and 7 November. Solzhenitsyn had been arrested at the

Artillery Captain Alexander Solzhenitsyn. Like countless other Soviet fighting men, his reward for war service was a term in the Gulag.

front by the NKVD three months earlier, accused of making disparaging remarks about Stalin. He was one of thousands of returning servicemen sent to the Gulag on suspicion of treachery.

'Above the muzzle of our window, and from all the other cells of the Lubyanka, and from all the windows of all the Moscow prisons, we, too, former prisoners of war and former front-line soldiers, watched the Moscow heavens, patterned with fireworks and criss-crossed by the beams of searchlights,' Solzhenitsyn wrote. 'That victory was not for us ...'

Twenty million Soviet citizens had died in the struggle. Thousands more were repatriated from the West, to face certain death under the provisions of the Yalta Agreement between Stalin, Churchill and Roosevelt. Captain Solzhenitsyn got an eight-year sentence. But the nightmare was not yet over. Stalinism, too, had eight more years to run.

The victory parade in Red Square, Moscow. Its high point came when Red Army troops dashed the standards of the defeated German regiments to the ground in front of Lenin's mausoleum.

6 Survivors

The Iron Curtain which fell across Europe as the war ended cut the old continent in two. In the Baltic republics, so recently swallowed into the Soviet Empire, optimists believed the Allied victory would return their national sovereignty. They were mistaken. In the wake of the victory parades came the tanks.

Vytautas Milvydas was a fifteen-year-old Lithuanian peasant boy whose brothers were already in hiding. His whole family were under orders for deportation when one night his brothers reappeared and took the boy into the woods. His life as a Forest Brother began. Their partisan band grew from four to thirty members, moving around at night, helped by loyal homesteaders, launching attacks on the NKVD troops who pursued them, and resisting the campaign of collectivization. They held out until their capture in 1949 sent them off to the Gulag.

Stalin at an election meeting at the Bolshoi Theatre in 1946. After the war, his public appearances became rarer. His health had begun to deteriorate and he took longer holidays.

The camps were filling up with sullen nationalists as well as returning frontline soldiers. It was an explosive mix. The late 1940s saw a succession of strikes and risings throughout the Gulag, bloodily repressed. The first was in the Arctic camps, led by Red Army officers who were all graduates of the Frunze Military Academy. They disarmed and killed their guards, liberated a neighbouring camp, and marched on the town of Vorkuta. Paratroopers and divebombers were sent against them.

The forties were a miserable time. Within a year of the end of the war, the collective farms were merged into huge units, private plots limited and state procurement prices dropped.

The result was another famine in the Ukraine. Nikita Khrushchev, party chief in the Ukraine, appealed to Stalin for help. Stalin replied: 'You're being soft-bellied! They're deceiving you! They're counting on being able to appeal to your sentimentality.'

Life in the cities was not much better. The fortunate lived in communal flats, rooms divided by blankets hanging from the ceiling, an entire family berthed on each side. The rest were accommodated in dugouts or barracks. State food prices were put up: the price of one kilo of black bread more than tripled. None of the draconian wartime labour laws were lifted, so workers were

Stalin at Potsdam in July 1945. At this conference with Churchill and US President Harry S. Truman, Stalin learned officially that the West had developed the atom bomb. In public Stalin said he did 'not consider the atomic bomb such a serious force'; in private he ordered Soviet scientists to 'hurry up the work' on their own version.

still moved around at the behest of the authorities, and penalized heavily for drinking or absenteeism. Most of the people evacuated to the Urals were not allowed back to their old homes. And in 1947, in an attempt to squash black marketeers and reduce inflationary pressure, an overnight currency reform wiped out the savings of millions.

There was a fierce cultural clampdown, too. Andrei Zhdanov, the clever but dogmatic Communist who had run Leningrad during the 900-day Nazi siege, launched an attack on two Leningrad authors. He accused the poet Anna Akhmatova of pessimism and decadence because she wrote love poems. The satirist Mikhail Zoshchenko was charged with rotten ideological nihilism, because of a short story in which a monkey escaped from a zoo, spent a day observing Soviet life and concluded captivity was more congenial. The composers Shostakovich and Prokofiev were attacked for failing to write melodies which could be whistled by a worker.

Scientists did not escape Zhdanov's ire. As in the arts, and among the returning soldiers sent to the camps, the charge was infection with Western bourgeois decadent ideas. University courses were rewritten and lecturers sacked, to bring studies into line with the fraudulent theories of Stalin's house biologist, Trofim Lysenko.

The poet Boris Pasternak, who had escaped the purges in spite of being Jewish and romantically inclined, had begun writing a novel critical of the revolution. 'I returned to my novel when I observed the thwarting of our hopes for postwar change,' he said. After he read out parts of the work in progress to a Moscow audience, in 1949 his pregnant lover, Olga Ivinskaya, was cruelly interrogated inside the Lubyanka prison. She lost the baby, and was sent to the camps. He continued writing *Doctor Zhivago* with Olga as the model for the heroine, Lara. Pasternak's hero Zhivago says in the novel: 'A grown man must grit his teeth and share his country's destiny.'

By the time Zhdanov died suddenly in 1948, his position may have been powerful enough to mount a challenge to Stalin's leadership. Retribution followed posthumously as the Leningrad Party organization was savagely purged. Hundreds of Party and soviet officials were executed as Stalin sought to regain control over this most independent-minded Russian city. Its disgrace was so complete that the city's heroic war record was laid aside. The Museum of the Defence of Leningrad was closed, its director arrested, and its archives confiscated.

Stalin's seventieth birthday was celebrated in 1949 with extraordinary pomp and adulation. Batteries of searchlights illuminated the night sky, picking out a gigantic portrait of him suspended over Moscow on a balloon. At a ceremony in the Bolshoi Theatre, the Chinese leader Mao Tse-tung sat at his right hand. At his left was Nikita Khrushchev, newly appointed Party

Andrei Zhdanov, described as the 'saviour of Leningrad' during the war, became the scourge of intellectuals after it. His campaign was directed against writers, artists and musicians whose work failed to conform to strict Party ideology.

The Stalin cult reaches new heights. A montage from Ogonyok *magazine showing the spectacular illuminated portrait of Stalin suspended over Red Square on his seventieth birthday in December 1949. The church joined in the celebrations with a prayer thanking God 'that He has given us this pillar of peace, Stalin, this pillar of social justice.'*

Огонёк

№ 52   ДЕКАБРЬ   1949
ИЗДАТЕЛЬСТВО «ПРАВДА»

leader in Moscow. *Pravda* ran to twelve pages rather than the usual four, and apart from two column inches of reports on the women's chess championship, the whole paper was devoted to articles in honour of Stalin.

By this time the Supreme Leader, Father of the People and Coryphaeus of the Sciences was an old and tired man. Increasingly, he complained to his daughter that he was lonely. He took to visiting the grave of his dead wife.

But there is evidence that even now he was planning a new purge. In January 1953, the most outlandish of all conspiracies was uncovered, at the very bedsides of the Kremlin chiefs. Moscow Radio announced that the Kremlin doctors were plotting to kill the country's leaders. They were 'killers in white coats' and 'rootless cosmopolitans' – a code, just as in Hitler's time, for Jews.

There were clear signs that anti-Semitism had been on the rise since the war. The actor Mikhoels, chairman of the wartime Jewish Anti-Fascist Committee, had seen Molotov in 1947 to complain about government discrimination. Soon afterwards the press announced Mikhoels' death. He was said to have been murdered by anti-Semites, but Stalin's daughter Svetlana Alliluyeva believes she heard her father arranging a motor accident for him. In 1949, all publications in Yiddish and the Yiddish Theatre were closed down.

The Doctors' Plot unleashed all the fury of Russian anti-Semitism. Dr Yakob Rapaport, a pathologist who at ninety is the last surviving victim of the plot, was arrested and taken to

BELOW LEFT *Dr Feldman, one of the Kremlin physicians accused in the 1953 Doctors' Plot. Stalin alleged they planned to murder top politicians, but his real purpose was to crack down on Jews. Khruschchev noticed how 'anti-Semitism grew like a growth inside Stalin's own brain'.*

BELOW *Stalin is thought to have ordered personally the mysterious death, in Minsk, of Solomon Mikhoels. The great actor of the Yiddish theatre was later denounced for working for Western intelligence through a 'corrupt Jewish bourgeois nationalist organization'.*

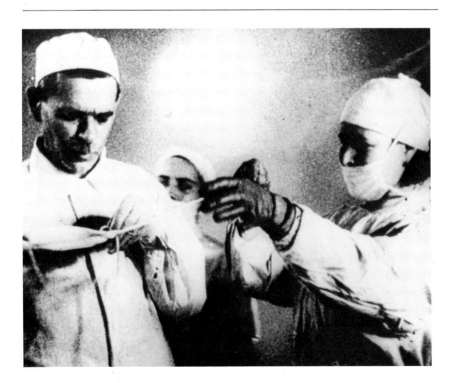

the Lubyanka. He remembers that people stopped taking their children to the doctor because they were afraid of being poisoned. His daughter Natalia was bullied by local boys who threw rotten vegetables and dead mice at her in the street. They said her father had taken pus from cancerous corpses and rubbed it into the skin of healthy Russians.

Rumours spread of a plan to deport all Jews to Siberia to make a fresh start. The newspapers simmered with hatred towards Jewish speculators and Zionist agents. And then on 2 March 1953, *Pravda* suddenly stopped being nasty about the Jews.

On 6 March came the announcement that Stalin was dead of a brain haemorrhage. He was seventy-three.

For countless millions, the death of their leader was a national tragedy. Crowds gathered in silent tribute, and Moscow was sealed off by the security forces. People died in the crush as the population queued in the cold to pay their last respects by the bier in the Hall of Columns. At night, Stalin's name was added to Lenin's above the mausoleum in Red Square, and the leader's body was laid to rest there.

In the Gulag, the Lithuanian partisan Vytautas Milvydas was working in the mines when all the lights went out. The prisoners waited in the dark for hours until eventually they were told: 'Our Father is dead.' Inside a month, the telephone was to ring at the flat where Natalia Rapaport and her mother waited. 'My darlings, it's me!' the doctor said. 'I am calling from the telephone booth downstairs. I didn't want you to faint at my sudden

Historians still argue about the precise circumstances of Stalin's death. Some say it was hastened by medical neglect; others that he was murdered. A grisly little drama is said to have followed the discovery of Stalin lying on the floor of his room. Frantic doctors applied leeches, and watched in horror as their patient stretched out his right arm, as though to speak, before death finally claimed him.

ABOVE *Stalin's lying-in-state. Within a decade, Khrushchev (left) was the only one left in government of all those featured with him in this photomontage. Secret police chief Lavrenty Beria (second left) was executed. Nikolai Bulganin (fourth left), Kliment Voroshilov and Lazar Kaganovich were all dismissed or forced to retire. Georgy Malenkov (third left) was sent to run a power station in Kazakhstan.*

LEFT *Proof that photo-faking did not die with Stalin. This picture was used to make the photomontage above. Khrushchev has been inserted into the most prominent position in place of Voroshilov, who has been moved to the right-hand side.*

appearance.' The Doctors' Plot was over, the doctors were freed, and twenty-five years of Stalinism were at an end.

The camps saw another wave of risings throughout the summer. Prisoners at Norilsk in Siberia, in Vorkuta, and at Kengir in Kazakhstan disarmed their guards and went on strike, demanding reexamination of their sentences, a shorter working day, better rations and the right to frequent correspondence and visits. In one Vorkuta camp, a non-violent protest was accompanied by banners bearing the words 'Coal for the fatherland, freedom for us', and a quote from Stalin: 'There is nothing more precious in the world than man himself.' In some camps conditions did improve. There are even reports of prisoners sending money or clothes to free relatives living on the grimmer collective farms.

In the immediate wake of the old leader's demise, Georgy Malenkov had replaced him at the head both of the Party and

In the Soviet Union, news of Stalin's death brought public displays of shock and grief. Elsewhere, reports were less respectful. In an Australian tabloid newspaper, 'Poor Old Joe!' headlined a story, datelined 'Heaven', which began: 'All hell broke out here today when the news flashed through by electronic telegraph that Joseph Stalin, 73, The Kremlin, Moscow, was on his way.'

The disgrace of the executed police chief Lavrenty Beria in 1953 was made known in a curious way. Owners of the Great Soviet Encyclopedia *were sent new pages to replace its entry on Beria. The substitute article was about the Bering Sea.*

of the government, and a faked photograph appeared in *Pravda* purporting to show him in a threesome with Stalin and Mao Tse-tung.

But within days, the rest of the leaders had put the brakes on. Collective leadership was now in order, and Malenkov had to give up one of his jobs. Beria, who was busy reorganizing his secret police, had brought his own troops into Moscow on the pretext of an outbreak of burglaries. The other leaders got together with the army generals and arrested Beria for 'anti-party and anti-state activities'. According to Khrushchev, he was shot on the spot to avoid any rescue attempt by troops loyal to him.

It was the last time the blood of a Party leader was spilt. The era of collective leadership had arrived. For a while all the top Party men went everywhere together, ostentatiously piling in and out of one official car to show their equality. Nobody expected this to last. The British ambassador Sir William Hayter freely admits that he was tipping Malenkov: but the winner was the little man with baggy trousers from the coal belt of the Ukraine.

Nikita Khrushchev was not a liberal. He was a ruthless and dedicated man who had many years of bloodshed on his conscience. But the waste and senseless cruelty of the Stalin years offended his energetic and optimistic nature. He became First

Western Kremlinologists in 1953 found this parade far less interesting . . .

. . . than watching Khrushchev and his colleagues in the collective leadership review the marchers from the Lenin Mausoleum. They hoped the line-up would show evidence of shifts in power and help them identify an individual leader.

Secretary of a party which now represented the elite of Soviet society from all walks of life, but which had lost its political influence under Stalin's control. The Party was, in effect, running everything but itself. Khrushchev was a reformer because he wanted to get the Party back to his own version of the Leninist ideal, and he wanted to be in charge.

The Twentieth Party Congress opened in February 1956. At Khrushchev's suggestion, delegates stood in memory of 'outstanding members of the Communist movement', including Stalin. But that was the end of the compliments. On the morning of 25 February, Khrushchev delivered his report, 'On the Cult of Personality and its Consequences', to a closed session of 1500 delegates. They were stunned as Khrushchev recited a litany of cruelty and mass repression.

The secret speech was not a secret for long. John Rettie, an English reporter working as Moscow correspondent for the Reuters news agency, got the scoop of his life when a KGB agent sat him down one long night and gave him the story. The headlines flashed round the world.

At meetings all over the Soviet Union, the Party faithful gathered in shock and pain to hear the speech read out by local officials. When Khrushchev himself addressed senior Party acti-

Khrushchev and Malenkov on a collective farm in 1954. Despite the failure of his programmes for replacing traditional crops with unsuitable ones like maize and melons, Khrushchev's enthusiasm for the exotic never diminished. In retirement at his dacha, he cultivated as many varieties of maize as he could find.

Trofim Lysenko, the charlatan scientist whose influence on both Stalin and Khrushchev caused havoc in the countryside and brought Soviet science into disrepute. His scheme to improve the growing properties of wheat and cotton proved fruitless. Equally harebrained was a plan to change the climate of the Russian steppes by planting vast numbers of oak trees.

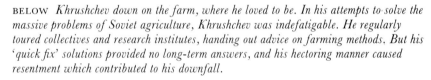

BELOW *Khrushchev down on the farm, where he loved to be. In his attempts to solve the massive problems of Soviet agriculture, Khrushchev was indefatigable. He regularly toured collectives and research institutes, handing out advice on farming methods. But his 'quick fix' solutions provided no long-term answers, and his hectoring manner caused resentment which contributed to his downfall.*

vists in Moscow, a note was sent to the platform demanding to know why he had allowed these crimes to happen. Khrushchev asked twice who had written the note. There was silence in the hall. Khrushchev said, 'The person who wrote this note is very afraid. We were afraid too.'

The rehabilitations began immediately. Special commissions were set up of three people: an official from the Prosecutor-General's office, a representative of the Central Committee and a Party member who had already been rehabilitated. They were invested with full powers to rehabilitate, issue pardons or reduce sentences in the name of the Supreme Soviet. By the summer of 1956, millions had been released.

Not all were pleased with the new conditions for prisoners. There were protests from the Interior Ministry, and at one session of the Supreme Soviet the government was criticized for 'health resort conditions' in the camps.

In Georgia, birthplace of the old dictator, national pride had been severely dented. On the third anniversary of his death, hundreds of students gathered at the statue of Stalin on the embankment near the river in Tbilisi. 'We were insulted as Georgians. We couldn't understand why this had suddenly happened,' remembers Givi Omiadze. 'We decided to march to the post office to send a telegram of protest to Molotov. I was in the front, and just as we got to the door the snipers opened fire.' Givi lost his leg in the shooting, and many young people died.

Polina Zhemchuzhina, Jewish wife of Foreign Minister Viacheslav Molotov, was one of the first Gulag prisoners released after Stalin's death. A victim of post-war anti-Semitism, she had been arrested as a Zionist spy after being seen talking in Hebrew to Israel's first ambassador to the Soviet Union, Golda Meir.

The Hotel Ukraine. One of the 'wedding cake' skyscrapers built in Moscow according to Stalin's architectural precepts. His pet project, the construction of the world's biggest building – a Palace of Soviets topped with a statue of Lenin one hundred metres high – came to nothing.

The Georgian riots were just the start. The fresh air of truth-telling blew westwards into the satellite state of Hungary, where the Soviet ambassador was a future Party leader, Yuri Andropov. On 23 October, thousands of young Hungarians wearing the red, white and green national cockade marched to Parliament Square in Budapest. That night they pulled down the huge statue of Stalin in the city park, and broke it up into souvenir-sized bits. Only the boots were left. The Russians dithered, but on 4 November, in the middle of the night, a thousand tanks entered the capital.

In the upper reaches of the Soviet party the Hungarian rising was seen as a disaster directly attributable to deStalinization. Many thought the policy played into the hands of the Western enemy. And nobody liked the way Khrushchev was using it to consolidate his own power.

In 1957, Khrushchev's rivals made a serious attempt to unseat him. Khrushchev, the consummate politician, packed a Central Committee meeting with his own supporters, flown in from all over the country with the help of the war hero Marshal Zhukov. He turned the tables on the plotters. Malenkov was sent to Kazakhstan to run a power station, and Molotov found himself Soviet ambassador to Outer Mongolia.

Hungary 1956. The statue of Stalin on Dozsa Gyorgy Street in Budapest is toppled and torn apart on the first night of the uprising. His bronze boots, left standing overnight, eventually succumbed to a metal-cutting machine.

The pace of deStalinization was not fast enough for the writers and artists who hoped for a new freedom of expression. Boris Pasternak had finished *Doctor Zhivago* in 1955, but could not get it published in the USSR. Then Sergio d'Angelo, an enterprising Italian representing the publishers Feltrinelli, turned up at the writer's dacha in the artistic colony of Peredelkino outside Moscow. As he handed over the manuscript, the author said: 'You've invited me to my own execution.'

The novel came off the press in Milan in November 1957. Within two years it had been translated into more than twenty languages and was a worldwide bestseller. Inside the Soviet Union it became one of the first books issued in *samizdat*, photographed page by page and read in secret.

On 23 October 1958, the Swedish Academy announced the award of the Nobel Prize for Literature to Boris Pasternak. He wired his response: 'Infinitely grateful, touched, proud, surprised, overwhelmed.' Hordes of foreign correspondents descended on the dacha to photograph the great man. Two days later the Kremlin revenge machine swung into action.

The first shot came from the *Literaturnaya Gazeta*, the official newspaper of the Writers Union, which featured a two-page spread of attacks. The book was accused of being decadent and artistically poverty-stricken. The author was a Judas who had libelled the October Revolution. The next day *Pravda* joined the fray. It described Pasternak as a self-infatuated Narcissus marooned in a literary backwater, a weed on Soviet soil. A day later the writer was thrown out of the union, which meant he could no longer work, and his lover Olga Ivinskaya lost all her translation contracts.

Pasternak cracked. He wired the Swedish Academy: 'In view of the meaning given to your award by the society to which I belong I must renounce this undeserved distinction which has been conferred upon me. Please do not take my voluntary renunciation amiss.'

He also wired the Central Committee: 'Have renounced Nobel Prize. Let Olga Ivinskaya work again.'

Terrified that he would be forcibly exiled from his homeland, already ill with the cancer which was to kill him in 1960, the elderly writer recanted publicly with a letter in *Pravda*.

Though the Soviet government attracted international opprobrium for its malicious treatment of Pasternak, it found itself ahead on scientific prestige. On Saturday, 5 October 1957, the Soviet Union won the first heat of the space race. The first Sputnik made a successful orbit of the earth 200 miles up in space, and its distinctive callsign became internationally recognizable. Robert Robinson, an American who had lived in the USSR for many years, remembers triumphant Russians coming up to him in the street and saying, 'Beep beep beep.'

Author Boris Pasternak was a victim of the post-war cultural clampdown. Although Zhdanov's death in 1948 brought some respite to the wider intellectual community, Pasternak's skirmishes with the authorities continued for another decade, culminating in the bitter row over the publication in the West of his novel Dr Zhivago.

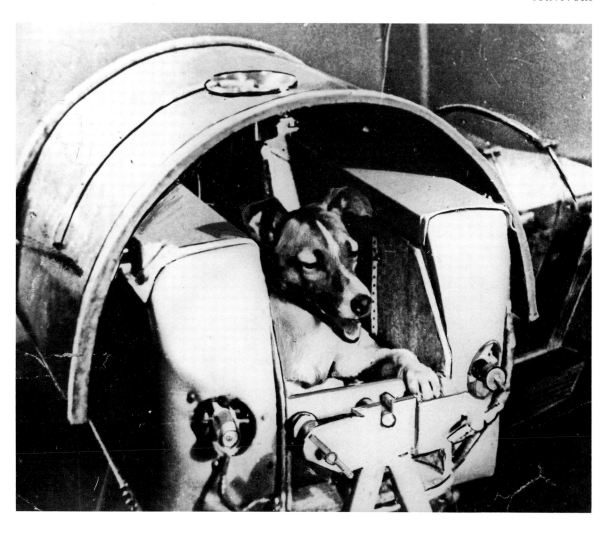

Laika the Soviet space dog was the first living creature in space. The mongrel's 'kennel' was a pressurized sphere in Sputnik 2, launched on 3 November 1957. Sadly, the spacecraft had no re-entry capsule and Laika faded away after seven days, when her oxygen supply ran out.

Sputnik's designer was Sergei Korolev, but he took none of the international glory. His identity was kept secret until his death in 1966, and his story is a classic of Soviet science.

Rocket research had begun in Russia in the early 1930s under the patronage of the Red Army general and Armaments Minister, Mikhail Tukhachevsky. But when Tukhachevsky was shot at the bloody height of the purges, all his projects were mothballed and his staff arrested. Sergei Korolev was one of the millions swept eastwards in 1937 by train and prison ship, and he found himself in the deadly camps of Kolyma. It was the gifted aircraft designer Tupolev who saved him. Tupolev had been purged, too, and locked up with his entire staff in a special prison called a *sharashka*. He got Korolev transferred, and there the country's leading aircraft and rocket engineers worked as prisoners all through the war.

Korolev was to be one of the hundreds of thousands of people rehabilitated in 1953 as soon as Stalin died. A new Ministry for

Medium Machine Building was set up under the eye of Leonid Brezhnev, with the specific job of organizing missile manufacture. It was a subject which at first went right over the heads of the Politburo, as Khrushchev admitted.

'When he showed us one of his rockets, we thought it looked like nothing but a huge cigar-shaped tube, and we didn't believe it would fly,' Khrushchev remembered. 'We were like peasants in a marketplace. We walked around the rocket, touching it, tapping it to see if it was sturdy enough – we did everything but lick it to see how it tasted.'

But Khrushchev soon came to believe fervently in Korolev's mysterious rockets. The new military hardware would need fewer soldiers, and its success would do wonders for his own position. The space programme became a public relations tool with which the canny First Secretary could raise his own prestige, save money, tame the Red Army, rattle a sabre at the United States, and bask in reflected glory. The programme was pushed ahead at breakneck speed.

Meanwhile, the much-vaunted collective leadership had vanished without trace. By 1958 Khrushchev was First Secretary of the Party and Chairman of the Council of Ministers – just as Stalin had been. He was also head of the new Supreme Defence Council. In other words, he now ran the party, the state and the armed forces. And he was becoming a globetrotting political superstar. On his return from the USA in September 1959, all the cinemas in the Soviet Union showed a long documentary of the tour, with America as the glossy background to an endless personal triumph.

In January 1960, Khrushchev decided to save money by demobilizing 1,200,000 servicemen. The Red Army commanders were not pleased.

In May of the same year, a Soviet rocket brought down an American U-2 spy plane over the Urals city of Sverdlovsk. The pilot, Gary Powers, bailed out and was caught by the KGB, to whom he immediately confessed that he was working for the Central Intelligence Agency. The affair was a huge embarrassment to Khrushchev. Western Kremlinologists, poring over the minutiae of phraseology in the Soviet press, noticed veiled criticism of the leader.

But within a year the Soviet Union scored the big one. On 12 April 1961, the spaceship *Vostok* was launched from the Baikonur Cosmodrome in Soviet Central Asia with a handsome young jet pilot at the helm. Yuri Gagarin was in flight for 108 minutes, flying across Siberia to deliver revolutionary greetings to countries below in South America and West Africa, before ejecting at 20,000 feet and descending in a parachute. He was welcomed back to Moscow as a national hero and greeted personally by Khrushchev.

For now Khrushchev's position looked secure. But the economy was still in a terrible state. In the eighteen months leading up to the Twenty-Second Party Congress, hundreds of officials and twenty members of the Central Committee lost their jobs in yet another wave of purges. The pretext was the embarrassing failure of Khrushchev's ambitious and frequently nonsensical agricultural policies.

Alexei Laryonov was First Secretary of the Party in Ryazan, a Hero of Socialist Labour because he had tripled the supply of meat from his region. In September 1960, Laryonov died. Within weeks the rumour began circulating that he had shot himself to avoid scandal.

It turned out that he had indeed tripled his supplies of meat – but only by slaughtering all his own region's cattle, including milch cows, and buying from surrounding regions too. Some of the meat was entirely fictional, some had been bought at high prices in state stores and gone through the books twice.

In the spring and summer of 1961, laws were passed which revived the death penalty for economic crimes like counterfeiting and trafficking in foreign currency. The law was applied retrospectively to Yan Rokotov, a Muscovite convicted of currency dealings. The unfortunate criminal was retried and shot on orders from above – the first of a hundred executions for economic crimes announced in the next two years. Though Party purges were now achieved without bloodshed, the same was not true of the clampdown on economic dishonesty among ordinary people.

As the Twenty-Second Congress met in the brand new Palace of Congresses inside the Kremlin walls, Khrushchev was determined

A simple sign announcing repairs camouflages preparations for the removal of Stalin's body from public display. That morning, 30 October 1961, the Twenty-Second Party Congress had decreed it 'inadmissible that the bier and body should remain in the Mausoleum of V. I. Lenin'.

Stalin's grave with its plain granite plaque. Although Stalin's coffin lay under tons of cement, the poet Yevtushenko asked the government:

'to double, to treble
the guards over that gravestone
   slab,
so that Stalin should not rise
   again,
and with Stalin – the past.'

once again to combine another dose of deStalinization with a clampdown against his rivals. The Twentieth Congress had mentioned only the victims of Stalinism: this time the spotlight was to be on the perpetrators.

First-time delegate Mikhail Gorbachev, thirty-year-old head of the Young Communist organization in his home town of Stavropol, was among those who heard the new charge – that Molotov, Kaganovich, Malenkov and Voroshilov bore personal responsibility for the repressions. 'How can these people sleep in peace?' asked their bitterest accuser, Shelepin, new head of the KGB. 'They must be haunted by nightmares, they must hear the sobs and curses of the mothers, wives and children of innocent comrades done to death.'

Two days before the end of the Congress, the former prisoner Lazurkina declared that she spoke to Vladimir Ilyich Lenin every day: 'Yesterday I consulted Ilyich as if he were alive in front of me, and he told me, "It is unpleasant for me to lie next to Stalin, who brought so much misfortune to the Party."' That very night the body was removed from the Mausoleum in Red Square and reburied. All cities, villages, collective farms and factories which bore his name were instructed to drop it. Stalingrad became Volgograd.

Meanwhile, the Congress was hearing adulatory speeches about the leader which sounded suspiciously familiar to those brought up in the Stalinist age.

'He displays endless activity ... tirelessly upholds the cause of peace and of freedom for all nations,' said Leonid Brezhnev. 'For all of us the daily activity of Nikita Sergeyevich Khrushchev is a magnificent example of tact and sympathy ... His inexhaustible energy, his revolutionary fervour, inspires us all to carry on the struggle.'

There was just one small harbinger of the defeat to come. 'The lessons of history must never be forgotten,' Alexei Kosygin warned the congress. 'There must be no place for the cult of personality in the building of communism.'

This Twenty-Second Party Congress, held in the year of Gagarin's triumph, proclaimed a victorious programme which declared that the stage of building socialism was now complete. The final stage, full communism, would be achieved within twenty years. So, by 1981, the Soviet people would be living in a world of peace and plenty, guided by the principle, 'From each according to his ability, to each according to his needs.' When that year came, two workers, Ivan Khakhulin and Ivan Provotorov, read this Party programme out in a public place. They got three and a half years in a camp for 'anti-Soviet propaganda'.

7 Prisoners of the Past

1962–1985

etalworker Petr Siuda, son of an Old Bolshevik who had perished in the purges, arrived at work on the first morning of June 1962 to find his comrades at the factory up in arms. Overnight it had been announced that the price of meat had gone up by 30 per cent. Petr remembers men who did not have enough kopecks in their pockets to buy dinner in the canteen. The workers were furious. By lunchtime the massive Novocherkassk Electric Engine Works was on strike.

What happened next in the old Don Cossack capital of Novocherkassk was hushed up for years. 'It was just like the 1905 or the February Revolutions,' milkman Vladimir Globa says. 'Workers out on the streets protesting about food prices, and soldiers shooting them down. I couldn't believe such a thing could happen in a socialist country.'

The strikers held meetings, and hung around, and complained, and laid plans for most of that hot first day of the crisis. That night there were arrests – Petr Siuda was among those who were

Khrushchev in the virgin lands of north Kazakhstan. Of all his agricultural schemes, his plan to put millions of acres of pastureland under intensive cultivation was the most ambitious.

rounded up, not to come home for years. Next morning the mood was militant. The workers decided to march on the local Party Committee office to present their protest. Tanks stood on the bridges as the demonstrators walked the several miles to the town centre, joined by more and more local people. When they reached Communist Party headquarters, they chanted and waved makeshift banners as troops guarded the doors. Children climbed into the trees in the pretty town square to get a better view.

Accounts of the next few minutes are confused. All agree that as the shooting began, the children in the trees began to drop like fruit to the ground. People remember seeing the body of the town hairdresser. To this day nobody knows how many died. The bodies are buried in unmarked graves in unknown places.

A week later, six KGB men came for Vladimir Globa. He served four years in Vorkuta. *Pravda* called for reinforcing the struggle 'against manifestations of bourgeois ideology, idleness, drunkenness and cupidity'. In the absence of any proper reporting, the Russian rumour machine went into overdrive. All over the country people talked in whispers of hundreds of deaths. In Novocherkassk itself the idea took hold that soldiers had gone into the local hospital and finished off the wounded. The truth has not been established. In May 1990, Petr Siuda died in mysterious circumstances while investigating the cover-up.

The background to that terrible day in Novocherkassk was Khrushchev's continued failure both to get to grips with the economy and to get his own way in the government.

Until Mikhail Gorbachev took his presidential powers in March 1990, no Soviet leader since Stalin has had sufficient individual force to impose his own ideas against the powerful lobbies at the top of Soviet politics. Khrushchev was determined to raise investment in farming and consumer goods, in order to improve people's standard of living, but he was continually frustrated in his attempts to reduce spending in two linked and crucial areas of the budget: the military and heavy industry. The traditionalists he contemptuously dubbed the 'steel-eaters' were always stronger.

Agriculture had been improving slowly, but Khrushchev's constant meddling and peculiar new ideas were not helping, especially when state procurement prices remained too low to encourage farmers to grow more. The economy stayed resolutely in a mess, its productivity declining.

Then, in May 1963, ecological disaster hit the virgin lands in Kazakhstan. Over-exploited in the first rush of enthusiasm, the thin soil was unprotected against hurricane-force winds which picked up millions of tonnes of topsoil and dumped it in the foothills of the Sayan Mountains. Six million hectares were lost for good.

Khrushchev was in trouble.

The United States used aerial photographs to justify the naval blockade of Cuba in October 1962. This photo shows a Soviet ship heading for the island with a cargo of missiles. Others revealed launch sites under construction.

ABOVE *Khrushchev's loud-mouthed barracking of speeches at the United Nations in 1960 caused a scandal. In the most notorious interruption of all, the Soviet leader beat the desk with a shoe. UN Secretary-General Dag Hammerskjold noticed that Khrushchev was wearing shoes on both feet at the time.*

LEFT *Khrushchev and US president John F. Kennedy. Years after the Cuban missile crisis, Khrushchev praised the American president in his memoirs. 'I'll always remember the late president with deep respect,' he wrote, 'because, in the final analysis, he showed himself to be sober-minded and determined to avoid war.'*

Groping for clues, Kremlinologists picked up the signs from reading the official *History of the Great Patriotic War*, which came out in five volumes between 1960 and 1963. Khrushchev was mentioned forty-one times in volume three, but only sixteen times in volume five.

Cuba was the final straw. On 22 October 1962, President John F. Kennedy announced to the world that he was to blockade the socialist Caribbean island of Cuba, where forty Russian nuclear missiles had been detected. A duel developed between the two superpowers that kept the Western world in terror of war, until Khrushchev climbed down.

The leader was in disgrace. The newspapers began to emphasize collective leadership again. The only town in the Soviet Union to bear his name suddenly changed it. But Khrushchev was not finished yet, and his rivals were still kept in check by his most potent weapon, the deStalinization policy.

The diplomatic fiasco had come hard on the heels of a remarkable summer of cultural thaw at home. Rumours were rife that a literary sensation was in the offing, and a fortnight after Cuba the magazine *Novy Mir* published a short story about labour camp life called 'One Day in the Life of Ivan Denisovich'. The author was Alexander Solzhenitsyn. Publication was sanctioned personally by Khrushchev. He was raising the stakes once again in his fight against 'the heirs of Stalin'.

His rivals did not take this lying down. On 1 December 1962,

Alexander Solzhenitsyn. Khrushchev persuaded the Central Committee to allow the publication of 'One Day in the Life of Ivan Denisovich' by getting them to read proof copies. The author found, however, that this did not guarantee publication of his other works. Solzhenitsyn was finally expelled from the country in February 1974 and later went to live in Vermont, USA.

Khrushchev visited an exhibition at the Manezh, the old tsarist riding school in Moscow. Two thousand paintings hung there, and the leader's minders made sure he took a look at the most abstract efforts. Right on cue, Khrushchev lost his temper. There was wild talk about the pictures looking like the contents of a baby's nappy, the daubings of a donkey's tail.

17 April 1964 was Khrushchev's seventieth birthday, and it was the occasion for one last great show of unity around him. Head of State Leonid Brezhnev awarded him a new Hero of the Soviet Union medal. In front of the television cameras, Khrushchev declared himself 'pleased with his life and destiny' and announced he had no intention of retiring. Six months later he was out.

He was on holiday in the Black Sea resort of Sochi when the telephone call came through. He got on a plane to Moscow and went straight to a meeting of the Party Presidium. The dour ideology chief Mikhail Suslov read an indictment of all his failings. Nobody spoke in his favour.

An editorial in *Pravda* said: 'Harebrained scheming, hasty conclusions, rash decisions and actions based on wishful thinking, boasting and empty words, bureaucratism, the refusal to take into account all the achievements of science and practical experience – all these defects are alien to the Party.'

Khrushchev had no power base outside his own subordinates. And it was his own team that overthrew him. After his enforced retirement, one of his grandsons was asked by a teacher what the old man did all day. 'Grandad cries,' the child said.

His successors' first concern was to gain acceptance from the one group they had not consulted – the population. They abolished the limitations Khrushchev had imposed on the size of peasants' individual plots, resumed the distribution of flour in the cities, and announced an extra New Year's Holiday. Then they began to mollify the powerful lobbies.

Khrushchev had upset the military and the 'steel-eaters' by promoting consumer goods. He had infuriated the agricultural sector by continually interfering. Party functionaries were fuming about their loss of job security since he had put a compulsory limit to how long they could serve. Economic managers wanted to get on with their jobs.

Within days of Khrushchev's fall, the technocratic new Prime Minister Alexei Kosygin told *Pravda*: 'We cannot hope to exceed the high productivity reached by the most developed capitalist countries unless we increase the workers' initiative and freedom of action.'

But those who hoped for genuine economic reform were to be disappointed. The Party was not yet capable of letting go. And the Party apparatchiks were tired of the years of carping about their past.

Khrushchev in retirement, 1967. According to Khrushchev's son Sergei, the first hint of his father's downfall three years earlier came when officials broke with tradition and failed to telephone him with news of a space launch.

ABOVE RIGHT *Nina Khrushchev bids her husband farewell at his funeral on 13 September 1971. Khrushchev had died two days earlier after a walk in the woods to gather mushrooms.*

In death, Khrushchev sprang one final surprise. In his will he asked that his monument in Moscow's Novodevichy cemetery should be carved by sculptor Ernst Neizvestny, whose work he had once denounced.

In May 1965, the country celebrated the twentieth anniversary
of the victory over Hitler. Stalin's name began to reappear, as
military reminiscences paid tribute to his wartime role. The
museum in his home town of Gori in Georgia reopened. In
Leningrad, the Party warned writers against losing sight of the
positive aspects of the Party's role in the 1930s. The term 'cult of
personality' disappeared from the press. The anniversary of the
Twentieth Congress went by without a mention.

Leonid Brezhnev was in the forefront of the partial rehabili-
tation of Stalin and the establishment of stable Party rule. He
was emerging as number one in the collective leadership, and
flattering accounts appeared of his exploits in hitherto unknown
wartime engagements. The man from Dneprodzherzinsk owed
his rise in the ranks entirely to Khrushchev, who had promoted
him steadily in the Ukraine from 1938 onwards. He was one of
those who benefited directly from the way the 'dead men's shoes'
effect was accelerated by the purges.

Soon Khrushchev's rule limiting the term of office for Party
officials was thrown out. Functionaries could breathe easily again.

*Leonid Brezhnev,
Khrushchev's successor, had
worked closely with the ousted
Party leader. Yet Brezhnev's
policies were soon revealed to
be very different. Relations
with the West cooled. And at
home he introduced a period of
stability inside the Party.*

Andrei Sinyavsky and Yuli Daniel on trial in February 1966. Daniel got five years in a labour camp and Sinyavsky seven. Among the letters of protest from all over the world was one from five Soviet academics. They complained that the trial and the way it was reported in their country's press 'did greater harm to the world Communist movement, to our country, our system and our ideology, than could have been inflicted by any number of anti-Communist novels ...'

After the terror of Stalin's reign, and the chaos of Khrushchev's, the Soviet Union was in for a period of stability, and that meant everybody kept their job and their perks for life. The Thaw was over. The KGB chief Semichastny urged the arrest of a thousand intellectuals in Moscow.

In September 1965, the satirists Andrei Sinyavsky and Yuli Daniel were arrested in the capital. Their trial on charges of spreading anti-Soviet propaganda, backed by crudely contrived evidence, became a major international embarrassment. Further humiliation followed when Stalin's daughter Svetlana Alliluyeva defected to the West. Brezhnev was furious. He sacked Semichastny, passed some more repressive laws and brought in a new KGB chief: Yuri Andropov. It was a brilliant appointment.

Andropov was a puritanical and dedicated Party loyalist. By diligent work and clear thinking, he was able to recreate the KGB into an elite corps skimming the cream of university graduates. He formed a new Chief Directorate, the Fifth, to exploit the differences between various elements of what the West was beginning to call the dissident movement. A past master of the art of divide and rule, he contained and marginalized dissent. The Jews had the best organized support in the West – he gave them almost three-quarters of a million exit visas. Particularly troublesome figures like Solzhenitsyn were deported. Camps and mental hospitals were used to contain and often destroy the most dangerous elements.

Party leaders were more than satisfied with a man who could make the KGB more efficient and still keep it on a strict Party

ABOVE *The case of Andrei Sakharov and his wife Yelena Bonner was an international human rights cause célèbre of the 1970s and 1980s. Sakharov, the 'father' of the Soviet hydrogen bomb, later called for a ban on nuclear weapons. He won the Nobel Peace Prize in 1975 for his courageous campaigns in the face of harassment from the authorities.*

ABOVE AND LEFT
Squashing dissent. In Red Square, Moscow, a woman named Agapova protests against the authorities' refusal to grant exit visas to members of her family. The sign she is carrying reads, 'Brezhnev, Let the Agapovs Go!' The second photograph shows the abrupt end to her demonstration. She is seized by a policeman and placed under arrest.

Jewish 'refuseniks' intensified their campaign for the right to emigrate to Israel after the Soviet Union declared its support for the Arab side in the 1967 Arab–Israeli war.

leash. Nobody wanted the secret police ever to regain the independence it had under Stalin and Beria. Brezhnev paid tribute in 1976: 'Our Party considers it an important principle that this keen weapon for the defence of the state's and people's security against the intrigues of the enemy should be in clean and unimpeachable hands.'

The most imaginative element of Andropov's strategy was a piece of thoroughly Western-style marketing. He set about transforming the image of the KGB. James Bond was the model for a spate of films and thriller novels about heroic secret police-men. Television serials kept the nation glued to its sofas.

Throughout this time, small dissenting voices continued to be heard. Natalia Gorbanevskaya and her friends got together in the kitchens of their flats in Moscow to act as the central post office for dissident thought and news. They started the *Chronicle of Current Events*, a regular beacon of carefully edited and factual reporting of the repression of human rights. People sat up late into the night typing copy after copy on the thinnest of onion-skin paper. A new word entered the English language as the undercover activities of the *samizdat* activists caught the imagination of Western correspondents.

There were amazing feats of cloak-and-dagger printing. The Evangelical Baptists had set up a complete underground publishing empire in 1966, after they were refused permission to print Bibles. The believers taught themselves all the skills and set their own type on a farm in Latvia, which was only discovered by helicopter after three years in operation. By 1983, they had published half a million Bibles in various languages.

Christians outside a prison camp in the Donetsk region of the Ukraine. They had fallen foul of the state's increasingly stringent curbs on religious activity. Khrushchev closed two-thirds of all Russian Orthodox churches, seven out of ten theological schools and almost all monasteries. Under Brezhnev, believers were in the forefront of the dissident movement.

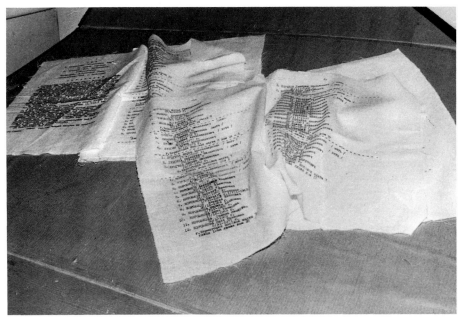

Church documents secretly printed on cotton sheets. In defiance of the authorities, complete books and articles were laboriously copied and circulated in samizdat *– the word means 'self-publishing'. In the 1970s, samizdat activists were often confined in psychiatric hospitals.*

Andropov did not turn the whole KGB over to squashing dissent. He also transformed the organization into an anti-corruption force. His man in Azerbaijan uncovered a web of bribery and privilege in the southern Muslim republic, where people had been buying and selling prestigious jobs. The going rate for a chief of police was 50,000 roubles, and the buyer soon cleared his investment through taking bribes. Geidar Aliev's investigation swept away the entire republican leadership, and his prize was a seat on the Politburo.

ABOVE *November 1967. Previously secret missiles are revealed during the parade to mark the fiftieth anniversary of the Revolution. Under Leonid Brezhnev, military spending rose to new heights.*

BELOW *Czechoslovakia, August 1968. Before setting out, Red Army soldiers had been told their task was to help the Czechs repel a German invasion. Some became disillusioned when they found themselves repressing supporters of the Dubček government's programme of political reforms.*

Working on the Baikal-Amur
Mainline Railway.
Successive governments have
spent billions of roubles trying
to complete this northern
alternative to the Trans-
Siberian. In spite of the
enthusiasm of its volunteer
Young Communist labour
force, the project was blighted
by engineering problems, and
has been described as a
monument to the 'era of
stagnation'.

Swapping records from the
West in a Moscow street.

In the neighbouring republic of Georgia, corruption was equally widespread. Local Party leader Edward Shevardnadze spent years trying to stamp it out, travelling in a bulletproof car because of death threats. What the Georgians wanted was free trade. Since the government denied them the chance, they took it from under the counter. The sunny and carefree southern republic became a centre of the burgeoning black economy.

Otar Lazishvili was the kind of rag-trade entrepreneur who would have become a millionaire in any other society. He came pretty near it even in the USSR. After serving fifteen years in prison he is now back in his home in the Georgian capital of Tbilisi, aged by his experiences, tired and bitter, but still claiming he did nothing wrong.

In his factories the workers cut and stitched the clothes required of them by the plan. After hours they used the offcuts of fabric to make bags. They sold the bags on the side, and very popular they were, turning up all over the Soviet Union. The system was highly productive. Nobody regarded it as thieving, the workers prospered, and everyone was happy that the plan was fulfilled. His defence lawyer Irakli Razmadze says: 'They should have given him a medal, not sent him to prison.' Lazishvili is now re-employed at his old factory. In the workshop hang posters of Lenin, Stalin and Gorbachev.

The KGB campaign against corruption was an undoubted success on its own terms. But the black market continued to flourish. Denied the legal freedom to turn an honest penny, the entrepreneurial, the greedy and the downright criminal used their imaginations.

By October 1985, *Izvestia* calculated that the black economy generated 7000 million roubles a year, and most observers believe that figure was wildly underestimated. For people without Party connections and Party privileges, it was the only source of car mechanics, plumbers and theatre tickets, let alone the Western jeans and fancy goods to which many aspired.

But outside the cities, far from the developing sophistication of the urban young with their jeans and rock music, the massive scale of semi-official corruption and bad management was ruining lives.

The state of the economy in Soviet Central Asia used to be called Comrade Brezhnev's 101st problem, so low on the list of priorities did it seem to appear. But the crisis which was building up in the poor and distant east was to reach to the heart of the First Family and create a scandal of epic proportions.

The cultivation of cotton in Central Asia had been controversial since the time of the First Five-Year Plan. Ikramov and Khod-zhayev, the two Uzbek party leaders put on trial with Bukharin in 1938, had argued against the requirements of the Plan for intensive culture of cotton in their republic. 'You can't eat cotton,' they insisted. Their fears that concentration on this cash crop would reduce Uzbekistan to the status of a colonial dependency were interpreted as bourgeois nationalism, and they were shot. What happened was worse than they could have imagined.

The cotton workers in Uzbekistan are employees on huge state farms, turning out millions of tons of cotton for use not just in clothing and medicine, but also in weapons manufacture. They became terrified pawns in a huge game of inflated plans and fictional production, discovered when scientists monitoring the photographs taken by a space satellite noticed thousands of square miles of desert where there should have been cotton.

The First Secretary of the Party in Uzbekistan was one Sharaf Rashidov, a godfather of the powerful local mafia right up until his death in 1983. Rashidov and his friends paid officials to turn a blind eye to their massive falsification of the cotton harvest. Among the functionaries they bribed was Yuri Churbanov, a First Deputy Minister of the Interior who happened to be married to Brezhnev's daughter Galina.

Ibrahim Buryev was a Party worker who was sent to prison for five years when he tried to investigate the great Uzbek cotton scam. 'It was really just a manifestation of how the whole Soviet economy worked,' he says.

Every year the republic is given a production target, which is supposed to be based on realistic figures garnered from the collective and state farms. Every year those targets have to rise, in line with the Soviet philosophy of planned economic growth. But by the early 1970s the republic had reached its physical limit.

In 1974, at the Party Cotton Congress, Brezhnev turned to Rashidov and said in front of the whole crowd: 'Sharaf, will there be five million tons or not?' Rashidov looked anxious, but said there would. Brezhnev said: 'Sharaf, if there isn't you will lose your job.'

To raise productivity in line with the plan, it had been decided to take land out of market gardening and put it into cotton. This reduced the peasants' ability to grow their own food, leaving them in tiny oases surrounded by vast cotton fields. At harvest time their homes could not escape the wholesale spraying of defoliants including Agent Orange, the highly dangerous chemical used by America against Vietnam. The peasants grew poorer and sicker. But the republic was still not making its targets. There were two options: tell Moscow the targets could not be met, or tell lies. The second option proved easier and more profitable.

A massive complex of payoffs grew up. Farms bribed warehouses to say nonexistent cotton had been delivered. Warehouses bribed factories. Party officials profited from cotton which existed only on paper. Local chieftains ran their farms and towns like medieval barons. But it is the way the money was laundered which caused the most human misery. Simple peasants were forced to sign chits to the effect that they had received more wages than they had. If they refused, they lost their jobs and the tiny plot of land they still had. When the charade began to come to light, hundreds of people ended up in the dock charged with fraud.

Cotton rules human lives in Central Asia. It has also caused environmental damage which scientists believe could be worse than the effects of the nuclear accident at Chernobyl. In dry Central Asia, the only water comes from the few rivers that feed the Aral Sea. This water was required for the cotton fields.

In 1975, Soviet satellites began to detect major storms, usually moving southwest over the agriculturally important delta of the Amu Dar'ya river. The storms were picking up salt and poisonous dust from the dried-up bottom of the shrinking Aral Sea, and depositing it a thousand miles away.

The former fishing port of Aralsk is now thirty miles from the water's edge. Fishing boats rust in the poisonous, salty, over-fertilized marshes left behind, and there are no jobs. The water local people drink is poisoned by the chemicals poured into the cotton fields upstream.

The disappearance of the sea was no surprise to Soviet scientists. It was all predicted in a plan of bizarre and surreal dimensions

The war in Afghanistan. One justification given for the invasion in December 1979 by 100,000 Soviet troops was the 'Brezhnev Doctrine'. This stated that the Soviet Union was entitled to use force to re-establish socialism in any country in which it appeared to be under attack.

ABOVE *The spectacular opening ceremony of the Moscow Olympic Games in the summer of 1980 was presided over by Leonid Brezhnev. The games were intended to show off Soviet sporting prowess and achievements to the world.*

LEFT *A boycott by the United States and other countries opposed to the invasion of Afghanistan cast a shadow over the games. Other sanctions used against the USSR included the suspension of international flights. The most serious consequence of the war, however, was the setback to detente between the superpowers.*

Leonid Brezhnev visiting West Germany in November 1981. In 1988, the Soviet historian Roy Medvedev claimed that the Soviet leader had been kept in power for six years after a serious stroke which had left him 'clinically dead'. The historian wrote: 'Gradually, Brezhnev found it more and more difficult to carry out the simplest of functions. He could no longer understand what was going on.'

At the funeral of Leonid Brezhnev in November 1982, his widow, Viktoria, is supported by members of her family. Brezhnev's death put paid to many of their careers.

in the late sixties, when Ministry of Water Resources engineers Konstantin Rakitin and Lev Litvak proposed a massive increase in the area of irrigated land. They realized that this would dry up the Aral Sea entirely, and therefore suggested their 'plan of the century'. They wanted to reverse the northward flow of two great Siberian rivers, to divert water from the Irtysh and the Ob through immense canals to the cotton fields of the south. The plan would demonstrate to the world the supremacy of Soviet engineering.

The rivers scheme was never begun. A growing conservation movement was protesting about the grandiose and destructive schemes dreamt up by the planners. But the shrinking of the Aral Sea can never now be arrested. Soviet conservationists describe it as an ecological black hole.

In European Russia at least, the Soviet people were at last beginning to benefit from their labours in building the world's second largest economy. When Brezhnev finally died in 1982, after several years of shuffling about half-dead from the effects of a stroke, nine out of every ten Soviet homes could watch his funeral on their own television. People were eating twice as much fish, butter and eggs. Unfortunately, they were also drinking four times as much alcohol.

The new leader was an abstemious man with a horror for the undisciplined and corrupt nature of much of Soviet life. Yuri Andropov was barely known in the West. The CIA were not even sure if his wife was still alive. US vice-president George Bush, a former head of the CIA, was one of scores of world government representatives gathered in the Kremlin for Brezhnev's funeral on 15 November 1982, agog to see the tall, stooping leader who at sixty-eight was the oldest man ever to take on the job.

Andropov had not been Brezhnev's choice. The old leader wanted the job to go to Konstantin Chernenko, an old friend from the 1950s. There was a third possible candidate, but at fifty-one the Agriculture Secretary Mikhail Gorbachev was ridiculously young.

One Friday afternoon soon afterwards, the workers at the Ordzhonikidze machine tool plant in Moscow got a shock as the new First Secretary bore down upon them on an unannounced tour of inspection. 'We must produce more goods to fill the shelves,' Andropov told them. 'Comrades, I'd like you to understand me correctly. Strengthening discipline is not just an issue for workers or engineers and technicians. It applies to everyone, starting with Ministers.'

Half a dozen elderly ministers got the sack. Before 1982 was out, the press was full of letters urging more discipline in the workplace, and the main television news showed workers complaining about drinking and lateness among fellow workers. In

Money and jewellery said to be some of the proceeds of the Uzbek cotton scandal are put on show by police. One estimate of the total sum involved was four billion roubles.

January 1983, local Party vigilantes in official red armbands started to search bath houses, hairdressers and cinemas, looking for people who ought to be at work. Many citizens were furious, especially those women caught standing in long queues to buy essentials.

But the discipline campaign carried on with tough new legislation against slackers, combined with cautious reforms designed to improve productivity in farms and factories by encouraging individual effort.

Andropov had been in power only a few months when it became clear that he was ailing. Kidney disease confined him to a special medical suite at the Kremlin hospital complex at Kuntsevo, west of Moscow. Only members of his family and selected officials were allowed to visit him there. Principal among the trusted aides allowed access to the sick man was Mikhail Gorbachev. It was an invaluable apprenticeship.

Andropov died in February 1984. There were two contenders this time: Gorbachev and the Leningrad party boss Grigory Romanov. It was a confused business. The Politburo and Central Committee gave the job to Chernenko as a stopgap, in the full

ABOVE *Yuri Churbanov on trial on corruption charges connected with the Uzbek cotton scandal. On the opening day of the case,* Pravda *described Churbanov and the others accused as 'guardians of the underworld' who pursued a path of 'degeneration and betrayal'.*

ABOVE *Andropov lies in state after his death in February 1984. The kidney disease which killed him was kept secret until the last moment. The usual explanation for his frequent absences from public occasions was that he was suffering from a cold.*

LEFT *When Yuri Andropov came to power, the Soviet leadership was still dominated by old men. He himself was sixty-eight. Yet, despite declining health, he continued the anti-corruption campaign he had begun while head of the KGB and began to make changes at top levels of the Party.*

The stopgap leader, Konstantin Chernenko (fifth from left), waves from the central stand of the Lenin mausoleum during the 1984 May Day parade. At the far right are the two rivals passed over in his favour, Mikhail Gorbachev and Grigory Romanov.

BELOW The death of Chernenko, after barely a year as leader, marked the end of the Brezhnev era. He had been Brezhnev's faithful assistant since the two of them had worked together in Moldavia in the late 1940s. Mikhail Gorbachev is second from left.

knowledge that the wheezing, white-haired old man was already in the advanced stages of emphysema. He was so weak and ill that he could not raise his hand to the coffin as Andropov's body was carried into Red Square.

That summer Mikhail and Raisa Gorbachev arrived in Britain to an ecstatic welcome. The energetic and charismatic Russian politician and his glamorous wife were the toast of a dazzled London press. Margaret Thatcher pronounced: 'I like Mr Gorbachev. We can do business together.'

When Chernenko died in March 1985, the succession appeared to the West to be a foregone conclusion. This was an illusion, of course. Gorbachev had plenty of enemies at the top of his Party. It was the sour-faced old Foreign Minister Andrei Gromyko who seems to have tipped the balance to ensure that Mikhail Gorbachev came into his heritage.

'Comrades,' Gromyko said, 'this man has a nice smile, but he has teeth of iron.'

A wall of remembrance on public display in Moscow reveals long-suppressed facts about the victims of Stalin. This is one of the ways in which the people of the Soviet Union are learning to come to terms with their traumatic past.

AFTERWORD: A Soviet Joke

The train of Communism is trundling across the field of life one day when the engine splutters and dies.

Comrade Stalin wakes up. 'Shoot the driver!' he suggests.

Comrade Khrushchev demurs. 'Rehabilitate the driver!' he argues.

Comrade Brezhnev settles comfortably back in his seat. 'Let's just pull the blinds down, close our eyes and rock from side to side,' he says. 'Then nobody will know the train has stopped.'

Finally Comrade Gorbachev leaps to his feet. 'You've all got it wrong!' he shouts. 'What we need to do is get off the train and all shout together: the train isn't working, the train isn't working . . .'

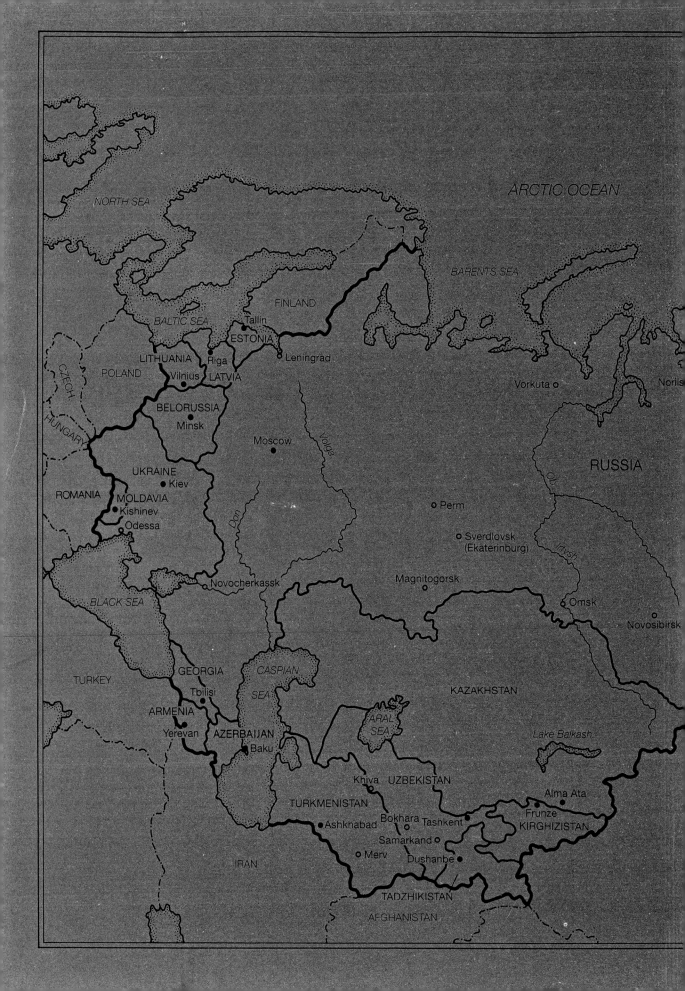